STUDIES ON FEMININITY

STUDIES ON FEMININITY

edited by

Alcira Mariam Alizade

A Volume in the Psychoanalysis & Women Series
for the Committee on Women and Psychoanalysis
of the International Psychoanalytical Association

KARNAC
LONDON   NEW YORK

First published in 2003 by
H. Karnac (Books) Ltd.
6 Pembroke Buildings, London NW10 6RE

British Library Cataloguing in Publication Data

A C.I.P. for this book is available from the British Library

ISBN 1 85575 957 8

10 9 8 7 6 5 4 3 2 1

Edited, designed, and produced by The Studio Publishing Services Ltd,
Exeter EX4 8JN

www.karnacbooks.com

CONTENTS

FOREWORD

COWAP, the Committee on Women and Psychoanalysis of the International Psychoanalytical Association, is both pleased and proud to present this second book, *Studies on Femininity*, of its series which provides a forum for discussion of issues involving sexuality, sexual identity, and gender constructs in a cross-cultural and international context.

The remit of the Committee is to investigate sexuality, interactions, and relationships between men and women. With this in mind, *Studies on Femininity* reviews certain theoretical and clinical conceptualizations of femininity and motherhood. Gender issues are considered in the frame of life periods (adolescence, adulthood, menopause).

In this volume, the reader will find not only papers from different essentialist, constructivist, and culture-based standpoints, but will also note the existence of theoretical and clinical intersections where psychoanalysis borders on closely-related disciplines.

Historically, sexuality, as viewed by psychoanalysis, is wide-ranging and encompasses heterogeneous forms that involve subjectivity, scenarios recorded in the psychic flesh, and inevitable psycho-physical and socio-cultural events.

In this book, classical areas of psychoanalysis are conjugated with postmodern questions and with new hypothesis to form a kind of heterogeneous, pluralistic spectrum defined to some extent by time and influenced by social factors that participate in the genesis and development of psychodynamics.

Maternal functions, as well as concepts of femininity, are outlined anew in an interplay of theoretical and clinical networks, with the aim of increasing the efficiency of analytic *praxis* freed from prejudice and monolithic convention.

The hope of the Committee is that these papers will encourage future volumes with the aim of opening up further pathways into psychoanalytic exploration.

Alcira Mariam Alizade
Chairperson,
Committee on Women and Psychoanalysis of the
International Psychoanalytical Association.

CONTRIBUTORS

Simona Argentieri Bondi is a training and supervising analyst of the Italian Psychoanalytical Association (AIPsi) and of the International Psychoanalytical Association. Her main scientific interests include the mind–body relationship, psychosomatic medicine, and gender identity and she has published extensively in these fields. Besides her full time clinical practice she has been involved in the field of bio-ethics, in teaching at Universities and in active psychoanalytic divulgation in the mass media. She has dedicated much thought to the relationship between psychoanalysis and culture and art, particularly the cinema. She is the author of many essays and books on the above subjects, including *Freud in Hollywood*, *The Babel of the Unconscious* and *The Maternal Father*.

Giangaetano Bartolomei, PhD, is a member of the Italian Psycho-analytic Society and works in private practice in Florence. He teaches Sociology of Knowledge at the University of Pisa.

Nancy J. Chodorow is professor of Sociology and clinical professor of Psychology at the University of California, Berkeley, faculty member of the San Francisco Psychoanalytic Institute, and in private practice in Oakland, CA. Her books include the award-winning *The Reproduction of Mothering*, *Feminism and Psychoanalytic Theory*, *Femininities, Masculinities, Sexualities*, and *The Power of Feelings* (winner of the L. Bryce Boyer Price). She is American Book Review Editor of *The International Journal of Psychoanalysis* and Associate Editor of *Studies in Gender and Sexuality*. She is recipient of the Distinguished Contributor Women and Psychoanalysis Award of Section 5 of Division 39. Her most recent fellowship was at the Radcliffe Institute for Advanced Study, Harvard, 2001–2002.

Monique Cournut-Janin is a psychiatrist and a training member of the Société Psychanalytique de Paris. She is a former coordinator of the Jean Favreau Consultation and Treatment Centre. In addition to her work as present training secretary of the S.P.P., she is a consultant member of the Committee on Women and Psychoanalysis of the International Psychoanalytical Association (COWAP). Among other texts, she has written *Féminin et Féminité* (1998).

Emma Piccioli, MD, is a member of the Italian Psychoanalytic Society and a training and supervising analyst. She works in private practice in Florence.

Danielle Quinodoz is a training analyst of the Swiss Psychoanalytical Society and works as a full-time adult psychoanalyst in private practice in Geneva. She was a Consultant in the Psychiatric Department of the Geneva University. She has published more than 40 psychoanalytical papers, mainly in the *International Journal of Psychoanalysis* and in the *Revue Française de Psychanalysis*. She is the author of *Emotional Vertigo, Between Anxiety and Pleasure* (1994) and *Words that Touch: A Psychoanalyst Learns to Speak* (2003). She was awarded the Sacerdoti Prize in 1989, and the "Prix Psychologie 1995" in Paris for her book on vertigo.

Teresa Rocha Leite Haudenschild is a training analyst and analyst of children and adolescents with the Brazilian Psychoanalytical Society of São Paulo, and full member of the International Psychoanalytical Association. She has been working in the field of clinical psychoanalysis for almost 30 years, particularly studying early symbolization and the constitution of identity, and has published in Brazilian, Latin-American and European journals and collections. She is currently a delegate of the COWAP in São Paulo, regional editor of the *Revista Brasileira de Psicanálise* (*Brazilian Psychoanalytic Journal*), and co-editor in the Publications Department of the São Paulo Psychoanalytical Society.

Gertraud Schlesinger-Kipp is a full member and training analyst of the German Psychoanalytical Association and the International Psychoanalytical Association. Since 1995, she has been head of the Alexander-Mitscherlich-Institute for Psychoanalysis and Psychotherapy in Kassel and has published widely in areas concerning psychotherapy with elderly patients, female identity and aging, psychodynamic aspects of climacteric change and menopause, gender and transference–counter-transference.

Frances Thomson-Salo is an adult and child psychoanalyst of the British Psychoanalytical Society, and a training analyst of the Australian Psychoanalytical Society. She works in private practice, and is a senior child psychotherapist at the Royal Children's Hospital, Melbourne, and a senior lecturer on the University of Melbourne Masters in Infant Mental Health. She has published on the topic of work with infants and children.

Matilde Ureta de Caplansky is a psychologist and psychoanalyst. She is a full member and training analyst of the Peruvian Society of Psychoanalysis. She is director of the School of Graduates of the Center of Psychoanalytic Psychotherapy of Lima, director and founder (1970–2000) of the Center of Psychosocial Development and Consultancy (CEDAPP), founder and member of the Group Therapy Association, Lima, Peru and co-chair for Latin America of the Committee on Women and Psychoanalysis (COWAP) of the International Psychoanalytical Association. She has been in clinical practice since 1970.

CHAPTER ONE

A particular kind of anxiety in women—it's nothing at all, really . . . (and doubly so)

Danielle Quinodoz

W hen I was studying a particular kind of vertigo in analysands of both sexes, the idea of a female equivalent of castration anxiety began to take shape in my mind. I had observed that "competition-related vertigo" (reflecting anxiety about surpassing a rival) was linked to castration anxiety in men (Quinodoz, 1994), and I wondered whether female analysands might have a similar kind of feeling. I then found myself faced with a dilemma: both male and female analysands do indeed seem to experience competition-related vertigo, yet, according to Freud, women can have a castration complex, but cannot experience castration anxiety. The question then began to take on a much more general significance that went far beyond the idea of vertigo: do women in fact experience anything that could be regarded as amounting to castration anxiety?

Freud's point of view: castration anxiety does not exist in women

In his lecture on "Anxiety and instinctual life", Freud discusses castration anxiety, and makes one very sensible comment: women do not have to fear losing an organ which they do not possess.

> Fear of castration is not, of course, the only motive for repression:
> indeed, it finds no place in women, for though they have a
> castration complex they cannot have a fear of being castrated. Its
> place is taken in their sex by a fear of loss of love, which is evidently
> a later prolongation of the infant's anxiety if it finds its mother
> absent. [1933, p. 87]

Thus the anxiety felt by women, when faced with the internal
demands of their libido, would not appear to imply an external
danger—the threat of being castrated—because, since they do not
possess a penis, they cannot fear that someone may come along and
cut it off.

Is the castration complex in women influenced only by penis envy?

Freud claims that the castration complex exists in both girls and
boys, but that its content differs according to the child's sex—the
young boy's experience is influenced by castration anxiety, while
for girls it is penis envy that plays the major role.

> [G]irls hold their mother responsible for their lack of a penis and do
> not forgive her for their being thus put at a disadvantage. [1933,
> p. 124]

Girls sometimes think that the desired penis will one day grow, or
that they may obtain one by some other means.

> [S]he continues to hold on for a long time to the wish to get
> something like it herself and she believes in that possibility for
> improbably long years; and analysis can show that, at a period
> when knowledge of reality has long since rejected the fulfilment of
> the wish as unattainable, it persists in the unconscious and retains a
> considerable cathexis of energy. [ibid., p. 125]

Analysis shows that the quest for success—for example, the wish for
a prestigious career—may sometimes be identified in such patients
as "a sublimated modification of this repressed wish" (ibid.).

The castration complex does not destroy the Oedipus complex in girls

According to Freud, awareness of the fact that she does not have a
penis makes the young girl feel she is of less value than her male

counterparts. This low self-esteem is then extended to women in general—and in particular to her mother. She then de-cathects the love she felt for her mother, thus allowing oedipal hostility to emerge. Disappointed at not having been given a penis by her mother, the young girl turns to her father in the hope that he will give her a baby, representing a substitute penis. "With the transference of the wish for a penis–baby on to her father, the girl has entered the situation of the Oedipus complex" (ibid., p. 129). The mother becomes the girl's rival, who receives from the father the penis–baby he refuses to give his daughter.

Freud then goes on to show that the development of the Oedipus complex in girls is, in some ways, the opposite of that in boys.

> The castration complex [in girls] prepares for the Oedipus complex instead of destroying it; the girl is driven out of her attachment to her mother through the influence of her envy for the penis and she enters the Oedipus situation as though into a haven of refuge. In the absence of fear of castration the chief motive is lacking which leads boys to surmount the Oedipus complex. Girls remain in it for an indeterminate length of time; they demolish it late and, even so, incompletely. [ibid.]

According to Freud, the man who turns away from his mother and towards his wife is relieved of his castration anxiety, while the woman who turns away from her father and towards her husband is not relieved of her penis envy; she still wants her husband to give her the penis–baby she used to demand from her father—the man's castration anxiety has disappeared, but not the woman's penis envy.

The female equivalent of castration anxiety

In my opinion, Freud's analysis of penis envy is important, as long as we bear in mind the fact that it is only a partial account. I am not the first person to think that Freud's analysis of the masculine complex and penis envy in girls focuses on only one aspect of feminine sexuality (Klein, 1928, 1932b; Chasseguet-Smirgel, 1964, pp. 129–130; McDougall, 1964, pp. 221–274; and many other psychoanalysts). Freud's account could give the impression that the absence of a penis is a typical feature of every woman's self-identity; this would lead us to think of a woman as being "a-man-without-a-penis", a sexless person who—as some women analysands put it—"has nothing". That would be tantamount to ignoring the fact that a woman cannot be defined simply as someone who does not have a male sex organ—she does possess a sex organ of her own, a female one. Of course, she may still experience penis envy, just as a man may feel envious with respect to the female sex organs and manifest a desire to give birth to children. However, a woman may also feel anxiety over losing her female sex organs, just as a man can experience castration anxiety.

In my view, though the young girl may not experience castration anxiety *stricto sensu*—anxiety about having a male sex organ removed—she does feels something similar: anxiety about losing her female genitals.

> The girl's very intense anxiety about her womanhood can be shown to be analogous to the boy's dread of castration, for it certainly contributes to the checking of her Oedipus impulses. [Klein, 1928, p. 195]

It's nothing at all, really . . . and doubly so

If the analyst fails to take into account the woman analysand's anxiety about losing her female sex organs, he may well put her in a difficult situation on two counts. Like every human being, she has to accept the fact that she cannot possess the "other" sex organ—this is the basic requirement for discovering one's own sex; but in addition, if her anxiety about losing "the sex organ she does have" is not taken into consideration, it is as though the very existence of these genitals were being denied or attributed to some negative hallucination or other. As Freud pointed out, we cannot lose something we do not possess; consequently, the failure to recognize that a woman might feel threatened as to the integrity of her female sex organs is equivalent to calling into question their very existence, thereby constituting just as much a threat of amputation as castration is for men. A woman may thus have the distressing experience of having "nothing at all, really . . . and doubly so": no male sex organ, but no female sex organ either.

In the course of psychoanalytic treatment, it becomes quite obvious just how serious are the consequences of denial or negative hallucination of the female sex organs in women analysands, who have the impression that human sexuality is defined in a positive sense purely by the presence of a penis. When such patients discover, in analysis, that, though they may not have a penis, they do have female genitals, they experience an enormous feeling of relief: they realize then that the fact of not having a penis gives them the advantage of having female organs and of desiring to receive (not *possess*) their partner's penis. They can at last admit how discredited they felt, given that "being without a penis" implied they were ripped apart, empty, a kind of nonentity.

The fact that the female sex organs are invisible (or only slightly visible) does not mean that the young girl is unaware of them. In addition to the possible role of proprioceptive perception of invisible organs, it is important to point out that there is a fantasy awareness of one's body image supported by the parents' reverie and by the kind of contact the immediate family has with the child. We are not talking here, of course, of a rational anatomical or physiological model based on external reality; it is a matter of internal representations of the body linked to unconscious bodily fantasies. These fantasies appear in adult analyses, and are expressed in a vivid way in the course of child analyses too.

I quite deliberately talk of threats to the female sex organs rather than to women's sense of self-identity. My purpose in so doing is to emphasize the fact that the sense of identity is anchored in the body, particularly in the sex organs and their functions. As Freud himself pointed out (1923, p. 26): "The ego is first and foremost a bodily ego". In every human being mental and bodily aspects are indissolubly linked and interdependent. This connection echoes Feud's idea of anaclisis (1905, pp. 181–182), when he emphasizes the close relationship between the sex drives and certain bodily functions. I should, all the same, make it clear that when I say "the body", I am in fact referring to fantasies and representations of the body, not to the actual body itself as an object of anatomical and physiological study.

That is why one's self-identity, as a woman or as a man, does not depend on the concrete existence of female or male sex organs. For each of us, it depends on how these organs are experienced in psychic reality, backed up by our fantasy knowledge of our body. If, because of some accident or illness, the sex organs of analysands have had to be operated on or amputated, these patients are no less men and women and still experience themselves as such. Similarly, a woman's self-identity is maintained, even after the menopause; indeed, often quite the opposite can be observed—a patient will have a better menopausal experience if her self-identity as a woman corresponds to her psychic reality rather than to her concrete anatomical and physiological one.

Some psychoanalysts prefer to use the term "phallus" to designate the symbolic character of the male sex organ, reserving the word "penis" for the anatomical and physiological organ itself. I myself prefer the word penis (and, *mutatis mutandis*, vagina and uterus) even when I am referring to symbolic functions and the bodily fantasies that accompany them. I quite deliberately avoid the term phallus since, for some psychoanalysts, it evokes the narcissistic omnipotence that can be ascribed to people of both sexes—hence the risk of generating misunderstanding whenever the term phallus is used. I accept that it is always possible to reach agreement on the symbolic sense we attach to any word in the language; but the word "phallus" is not neutral—in the original Greek, *phallos* designates a figurative representation of the male sex organ. In my view, were we to use the word to refer to what Lacanian analysts call "the signifier of desire", attributable indiscriminately to people of both sexes to indicate a narcissistic dimension, neither its original sense nor the precise bodily representation it echoes would be taken into account. By using the words I use, my idea is to emphasize the fact that drives, desires, and the whole of sexual and emotional life in general are ultimately rooted in the body.

The mother–daughter conflict

One of the consequences that anxiety about losing the female genitals brings in its wake is the twofold hostility that women analysands feel towards their mother for having failed to provide them with either male or female sex organs. The young girl feels not only her own self to be of little value, but also the image she has of her mother.

This mother–daughter conflict, which is both oedipal and pre-oedipal in nature, influences how the patient will come to see herself as a mother. She will tend to look on her children—real or symbolic, present in actual fact or only a future prospect—as penis–babies, as substitutes for her absent manliness and as narcissistic extensions of her self. The point at which children leave such a mother to live their own lives is a moment of high drama: she feels a part of her is being cut off, so that henceforth she will be without a penis. When the children are seen as independent human beings, their departure is a completely different experience: since the mother does not need them to buttress her feelings of self-identity, she does not lose a part of herself when they leave home—the sadness that accompanies any separation is of course still present, but there is much less anxiety in the mother about losing part of herself and consequently much less guilt in the child.

Once the analyst acknowledges the young girl's anxiety concerning her feminine riches, the oedipal situation can be seen from a different angle from that which Freud envisaged: girls find themselves in much the same situation as do boys. In her competition with mother to conquer father, the young girl does indeed feel threatened that, in revenge, something will be taken away from her—but this "something" is her female sex organs, not a penis. The anxiety is that of being amputated by the oedipal rival, the mother. The threat to her femininity can come in various guises, more or less psychic, more or less bodily.

Different ways of attacking the female genitals

I have observed, in my patients, that what unconsciously poses the worst threat to their self-identity as women is not, in fact, the possibility of having their sex organs amputated—because in this case there is at least a representation of the female genitals. Anxiety is much more intense when women are unaware of the existence of their sex organs: these are not felt to be in danger, because the patient has no representation of them as a result not only of repression, but also—and above all—of denial. This is an unconscious attack that remains covert. This type of destructiveness can be found even in analysands whose intellectual knowledge of the difference between the sexes is highly developed. However, in spite of all their erudition, there is no bodily fantasy or representation of their interior to accompany their feeling of self-identity as women.

In my view, there exists another kind of covert and destructive attack—removing all form of life, in fantasy, from the female sex organs. To put it another way, they are represented as an inanimate "thing"—for example, as a vase. To make this kind of attack a little clearer, I shall show how, in analysis, male and female patients can develop their representations of the container into something gradually more integrated.

The evolution of the containing function

In analysis, developments in the psychic knowledge that men and women have of male and female sexuality (both go together) can be observed thanks to their representations of the female body; initially, it can be represented as ripped open, with the female genitals being thought of as a hole (nothing, an orifice through which the body empties itself and which has no capacity for containing anything at all), thus expressing the absence of any organ whatsoever.

That said, representations of the female body may perhaps be slightly less denigrating—though still fired with hostility: the female genitals are seen as a cavity or lifeless thing-like container, such as a pot, a hollow, or a vase. Compared to the hole-fantasy, this representation at least designates a container that can hold something inside. It is still humiliating, however, because it suppresses all liveliness and any possibility of communication with whatever is contained in it or indeed with the whole person. It is, in fact, quite pernicious in that it is sometimes conveyed via idealized images that hide the aggression under the appearance of enhancing its value. For example, a patient (male or female), who represents the female sex organs as precious vases or jewel-boxes, seems to be holding them in high esteem—yet, underneath this apparent enhancement, a female patient will be sensitive to the fact that the symbolism really expresses the loss of any form of liveliness as regards her genitals. Indeed, she may well feel all the more distressed, because the unconscious attack is made to look like flattery.

Patients' attitudes change completely once they have a representation of the female genitals as a living hollow organ that can take inside, contain, and expel. This active organ is a far cry from the image of the vase that could only passively allow something in. We now have an organ which is an integral part of the whole person, which has a complex relationship with whatever it takes in, and which participates in creative activity. Together with these developing representations of the female genitals, the male sex organ is also represented in a more and more sophisticated way—penetration by the male organ has no meaning in terms of object relations if it is seen merely as taking place into a hole or a vase, however precious the latter may be stated to be.

The bodily fantasy that underlies the analysand's containing function takes on an even higher degree of symbolic value when the container is seen as relating to the mind. Henceforth, "containing" can be understood in terms of "making meaningful". A mother can contain her child's anxieties by making them meaningful; in so doing she becomes a good container for the child. That is why psychic bisexuality is so important: both father and mother can make their child's anxieties meaningful and thereby contain them. Consequently, the idea of the container no longer needs to be underpinned by any specific form—it need not, for example, be represented by a hollow shape, because an internal force is sufficient for holding things together: the penis, just as well as the uterus and the vagina, can be the basis for a containing function and symbolize the ability to make meaningful. Everyone, man or woman, can function as a psychic container according to his or her own pattern, be it male or female.

As early as 1993, I stated that, in my view, it was important to recognize that women could have an experience equivalent to castration anxiety (Quinodoz, 1993). A few years later, Godfrind (2001) came to the same conclusion, and spoke of "the female form of castration anxiety"; she did not, however, emphasize one point that I find extremely important, namely the difference between a lifeless container and an active one. In my view, if the analyst is not very careful, a female patient may well come to the conclusion that her analyst finds it quite all right for the female sex organs to be represented by a lifeless object—and the analyst could then be experienced, unconsciously, as colluding in the amputation of the female genitals. If the analyst fails to interpret the transference fear with respect to all liveliness being removed from her genitals, the patient may feel unable to trust this person who leaves her all alone to face up to the anxiety about being "nothing at all".

It is interesting to note that it is not only feminine attributes that can be turned into "things" (vase, jewel-box, etc.), but also masculine features (flagpole, sceptre, etc.), and that the threat to remove any kind of liveliness from these qualities hangs over both sexes. I want to make it clear, however, that I am not referring here to any universal meaning of symbolic images, but to the individual symbolic meaning that each patient gives to these images: the same symbol may mean disparagement or enhancement, depending on the fantasy life of the individual concerned.

The intimate relationship between mother and daughter: constructive homosexuality

During analysis, it is not only the mother–daughter conflict that is reactivated in the transference, but also the need for an intimate relationship between them. The young girl needs to discover that she is a woman through the relationship with her father, and at the same time needs to identify with her genital mother, perhaps in several different modes. I am thinking especially of a young woman patient who, in her initial analysis with a male analyst, had begun to develop her feminine aspects to their full potential, thanks to the opportunity she had in the transference to work through her oedipal desires with respect to her father. Some years later, however, she again found herself in difficulty, and came to me for further analysis. What appeared in this second analysis was not so much her rivalry with the analyst–mother, as the coexistence of rivalry and the strong wish for an intimate relationship with a desired mother. This wish was expressed in a twofold manner: the desire to combine with the pregenital mother, and also the longing for intimacy with the genital mother who would, for example—this was expressed in one of the patient's dreams—caress the daughter's breasts in order to make them grow. The patient needed me to reconstruct with her, in the transference, fantasies that expressed her desire to discover her own femininity in contact with the mother's body. Unable to deal with such fantasies on her own, she needed the analyst's capacity for reverie to make sense of her desires and to allow her to discover the constructive aspect of what appeared to her to be culpable homosexual tendencies. This was, in fact, a normal form of constructive homosexuality similar to the one we encounter in male patients, who have to acknowledge their passive desires for the father before discovering their own masculine strength.

Being precise about fantasizing the body

In my view, it is important for psychoanalysts to be very clear-cut in the way they formulate their interpretations. The feeling that the female genitals are "hidden" may tend to mean that they are mentioned in a very vague manner or perhaps even not at all, as if by using an imprecise form of words they would remain out of sight. For boys, the term "castration anxiety" exists, but there is nothing to express "the anxiety about having the female sex organs amputated". Interpretations will differ widely, depending on the type of anxiety a woman patient is experiencing. In some cases, there is a global feeling that they lack femininity; such patients have no idea how their self-identity as a whole—body and mind indissolubly linked—could be said to be feminine or not. In analysis, they will have to reconstruct their fantasy body almost from scratch. In other cases, the feeling that something is lacking is much more focused; in analysis, these patients may come to realize that they had no bodily fantasies about certain female organs— some remained non-existent, while others were felt to be "alive". One of my patients was surprised when she realized that inside her body was what she called a "baby room"; up till then, she had been aware only of the existence in fantasy of her vagina. Other patients have made the opposite discovery. When such moments occur during analysis, they are charged with emotion; patients begin to have much more subtle fantasies concerning the inside of their bodies. Awareness of differences between the organs used for digestion, excretion, and sexuality leads to a much more sophisticated synthesis of partial drives under the aegis of genital sexuality.

Clinical manifestations of anxiety about the double "nothing"

Here are some examples of the way in which women patients may express their anxiety about being amputated of their feminine characteristics: the feeling that they can never be attractive, that they will never be able to have children, biologically or symbolically, sterility, inability to have an orgasm, inhibition of curiosity, real or mental impoverishment, the compulsion to repeat an oedipal scenario in which the patient either constantly gives up her partner to the mother-rival or, on the contrary, is single-minded in wanting to rob the latter of hers, etc. Whatever form the distress actually takes, the patient always has the feeling of being empty, impoverished, and bereft of all riches.

When a patient, young or not-so-young, claims that "she will never find a husband", this is sometimes a way of expressing her anxiety about her female genitals—the organs that enable her to give a positive response to a partner—being removed or otherwise damaged. In the mind, this echoes the feeling of being deprived of the mental capacity for love. In some patients, this anxiety focuses specifically on the child-bearing organs; such patients may rush into a series of casual sexual encounters, sometimes with short-lived pregnancies followed by abortions, with the unconscious aim of verifying the fact that they do indeed have female sex organs which are perfectly capable of functioning correctly (Quinodoz, 1990). Some analysands may thus have conscious or unconscious guilt feelings linked to these distressing experiences; others have recourse to splitting mechanisms that limit their potentialities and are astonished when, in the course of the analysis, they get back into touch with "moments" that had completely disappeared from their lives. These patients feel very relieved when they discover that the experiences they had felt to be impossible to integrate are in fact meaningful.

Penis envy and anxiety about having the female genitals amputated are not mutually exclusive

The female equivalent of castration anxiety becomes more compli- cated when it combines with penis envy. From this perspective, the rival that the patient fears surpassing is equipped with a penis.

Unconsciously, the patient feels that if she is successful in life, this will be attributed by others in her immediate circle as due to a replacement penis; she fears that it will all be considered a trick and that other people will mockingly think: "She'd like us to believe she has a penis!" Such patients feel that they are doubly amputated: not only have they not been given the penis they so much desired, but they do not have female sex organs either. They have "nothing, really"—and doubly so . . .

In the exploratory interviews with one of my patients, she gave me the impression of being poor, impoverished, poverty-stricken . . . "Unconsciously, she made herself look like such a poor woman that I could not have brought myself to steal any of the riches she appeared not to have" (Quinodoz, 2002, pp. 152–159). In fact, the external poverty she exhibited echoed her inner misery, and unconsciously she needed me to believe in this. The inhibition of her feelings of possessing riches was her way of defending herself against the danger of entering into any kind of competition with her mother, and at the same time her apparent poverty was a symptom that involved penis envy. The alarm bells went off whenever the patient feared that any apparent riches she might have would be taken to be a substitute for manliness.

If castration anxiety has a female equivalent, might not the castration complex also have one?

We saw at the beginning of this chapter that, for Freud, though girls do not experience castration *anxiety*, they do have a castration *complex* just as boys do. In my view, there is not only an equivalent form of castration anxiety in women, but there exists also an equivalent form of the castration complex, generated by the anxiety over having the female genitals removed and by the desire to preserve these organs. I would call it the "female genitalia amputation complex". In addition, I would say that it is not only in girls that it seems to me impossible to do without the female genitalia amputation complex, with its anxiety specifically focused on the female sex organs; I think the same complex exists in boys also.

It remains the case, all the same, that feelings concerning the female genitals (the girl's anxiety about having them removed, the boy's envy of them, and the amputation complex involving them) are generally speaking less obvious than those that have to do with the male organs (the boy's castration anxiety, the girl's penis envy, and the castration complex). Yet I do not believe that the female genitalia amputation complex has less of a structural impact than the castration complex. I believe, too, that if the problems generated by this complex have not been properly worked through, the young girl will find it difficult to resolve her Oedipus complex properly, and the young boy's resolution of it will be incomplete. As Freud himself said in his report of the Little Hans case:

> If matters had lain entirely in my hands, I should have ventured to give the child the one remaining piece of enlightenment which his parents withheld from him. I should have confirmed his instinctive premonitions, by telling him of the existence of the vagina and of copulation; thus I should have still further diminished his unsolved residue, and put an end to his stream of questions. [Freud, 1909]

Even though Freud did not go on to develop his thoughts on the question, it seems to me that he was well aware of the importance— especially for boys—of the child's intuitive knowledge of the female genitals, and of the damage that might result were they to remain unmentioned.

CHAPTER TWO

The first lipstick:
the fear of femininity in parents of
adolescent girls[1]

Monique Cournut-Janin

A t the end of her school day, 15-year-old Marie came to the adolescent walk-in centre and said she had no intention of returning home. She wanted to be put up for the night and a place to be found for her, as soon as possible, in a hostel. After talking things over with the staff, Marie agreed that someone should phone her parents to inform them of her whereabouts, reassure them, and suggest that they come to see her the next day. During that telephone conversation, Marie's mother, in despair, cried out: "If she doesn't come back home, I'll kill myself", to which her father very angrily replied: "If she doesn't come back home, I'll kill her".

With these two sentences at the back of our minds, I would like to explore a situation that is not simply that of an adolescent girl at a crucial stage of her development, but that of a three-way crisis involving the parents of a young girl who is now an adolescent. In a more direct manner than for boys, this situation illustrates the classic theoretical questions concerning repudiation of femininity, as expressed in Freud's impeccably-argued discussion in the final chapter of "Analysis Terminable and Interminable" (Freud, 1937).

It is, of course, true that the moment when their daughter

reaches adolescence is not the only opportunity that the parental couple have to make structural adjustments to their psychological dynamics and economics; however, this event is so crucial and systematic that we may look upon these adjustments as one of the parameters of the adolescent crisis itself—which could be defined as a complex set of identificatory and object-related interactions that create connections or disconnections between the various protagonists, either unobtrusively or in a more spectacular fashion.

My hypotheses are based on my analytical work with adults, who are themselves parents, as well as with adolescents; a more direct and immediate light was thrown—sometimes brutally—on my thinking when I began to undertake therapeutic consultations with adolescents and support meetings with their parents (it was in such circumstances that I met Marie). The explosive nature of the crisis, with its acted-out high drama and overtones of an emergency, emphasizes and amplifies the fundamental parameters that, in my view, are present in every parent whose daughter is or is about to become adolescent. It is a crisis not only for the teenager, male or female, directly involved, but also for the parents, in that it turns their whole mind-set upside down. The tacit and unconscious consensus around a shared latency period breaks down, and the classic pattern is reversed: the children are now in the bedroom and the parents are on the other side—but just on the other side—of the door. The parents are the ones who, assailed by doubt, try to work out, as well as they can, *parental* sexual theories; like their infantile counterparts, these are neither true nor false, but they do indicate that fantasy representations as a whole are focused on an abruptly-reactivated primal scene. No storks, perhaps, nor babies purchased from the local department store, but, much more bluntly, rape and prostitution—topics that involve not only incestuous fantasies but also, and in a considerably more subtle manner, adjustments in identification.

Marie's parents owned a little restaurant in one of the outlying *arrondissements* of Paris. Mother did the cooking, father took charge of the bar. When Marie finished her day at school, she helped out as a waitress. Until fairly recently, business was good and theirs was just an ordinary family ... But not so long ago, as Marie said in a calm and composed tone of voice, she had become a bit defiant, because her father would not let her go out on dates, to the cinema or to the swimming-pool. She neatly pointed out the contradiction: "He wants me to be a waitress in his restaurant, where there are plenty of guys who make all kinds of comments about me, yet he won't let me spend an evening out with my friends, the rest of the girls. He criticizes me because I wear a mini-skirt and put on lipstick". She ended by throwing the ball back into her father's side of the court: "He'll have to make up his mind, one way or the other!"

Marie was a dark-haired girl, not very tall and slightly overweight. Her face was still child-like, but, a few months previously, her figure began unequivocally to take on the appearance of a pubertal adolescent ... A good achiever in school, she wanted to continue her studies, though she was not at that point sure in what field. She was not in any way in outright revolt against her family; she had a specific problem with her father that had recently become sufficiently important for her to decide, regretfully but firmly, to live elsewhere—i.e. in a hostel—in order to put an end to the "repeated scenes" her father subjected her to every evening. A friend of hers had told her about the walk-in centre[2]; Marie had decided to run away from home and seek help in a highly organized manner. She saw this as being both moral support "because it's not easy to leave your parents when you really like them a lot" and practical assistance in finding a hostel not too far away from her high school or from her family, because she intended to visit them every Sunday, the day the restaurant was closed.

Once they got over their initial explosive reactions, Marie's parents agreed to come to the Centre the following day. As was to be expected, it was her father who set the tone: anger, threats, bitter remonstrations of all kinds against his daughter, the Centre, society as a whole, etc. Passive and worn-out, Marie's mother sat quietly weeping.

After many discussions, together and separately, spread out over several days, we managed, more or less, to take some of the tension out of Marie's running away from home and the conflicts they had together. The solution she had imagined seemed difficult to put into practice; also, was it really logical to endorse a separation now that fantasies of murder and suicide appeared to be on the decrease? Each of them made an effort, and finally a compromise solution was reached: Marie was to return home, her father was to be more reasonable, her mother more joyful, and a specialized youth worker was to be assigned to the family to help them through this difficult phase. A year later, Marie came back to the Centre on a friendly visit, saying: "It's still pretty lively at home, but at least my father's less of a pain in the arse ..."

A very ordinary case, when all is said and done, with no sign of serious symptoms or declared psychopathology. But it is precisely because the situation *is* so ordinary that it is exemplary and worthy of comment on several different levels.

Even though the parental response in this case may have been somewhat extravagant, it was not tied in any specific way to Marie's running away from home. The fact that she did run off only revealed what was going on inside their minds, and projected it outside—and this is what I intend to explore, leaving Marie's escapade to one side, as a piece of symptomatic materialization. The same is true of the general atmosphere of their home circumstances and lifestyle: these too have to be kept in perspective. When a daughter goes through an adolescent crisis, families that have a strong and enduring traditional background—whether they belong to the old Catholic bourgeoisie in France or are of North African origin, to name but two examples—are quite often protected by the kind of tradition that, handed down from generation to generation, decides how the family wealth and inheritance is to be disposed of, or provides for marriages with their concomitant structures of kinship and lines of descent. For example, a planned marriage between a daughter and the son of the father's brother, like the decision to combine inherited wealth and shareholdings, ensures that a certain symbolic order is preserved, that the "family corpus" remains intact, and that the homosexual community of the menfolk who possess the wealth and the women of the family is solidly linked together. When it so happens that this kind of organization breaks down, the dramatic nature of the collapse is heightened. Misalliances and scandals deprive the parents of their cultural armour and force them to take another—shamefaced—look at their own personal difficulties.

I would add that these seem all the more exposed now that contraception has removed another screen behind which they could be camouflaged. The pill and voluntary termination of pregnancy have made somewhat null and void any lingering fears of unwanted pregnancies and the social disgrace that once attached to unmarried mothers. Now that the problem for parents is no longer there, it tends to emerge at its true level: whereas they thought they were still looking at a young girl, a woman now appears on the scene.

I should point out, of course, that there is no unique type of crisis, be it for the adolescent girl or for her parents. Each of the protagonists has to go through it and to cope with it according to his or her inner capacities, past history, and mental functioning. In the parents, for example, there is often a partial lifting of amnesia and a reactivation of repressed aspects of their own childhood. When their manner of functioning is based, above all, on counter-cathexis, these suddenly begin to fall apart, hence the explosion of violent affects and powerful drive-related impulses. In other cases, aspects that the parent had been unable to repress, counter-cathect or otherwise process in childhood or at puberty break into consciousness in the form of a traumatism which so overwhelms the protective shield against excitation that serious disorders or even somatic illnesses may occur. Given these different patterns of mental functioning and the variety of the actual situations that have to be coped with, what seems important is the distressing chain-reaction emergence of deferred phenomena suddenly reactivating earlier problem situations that, having remained to some extent unprocessed, now take on new meaning in a way that is experienced as more or less tolerable.

Each parent is subjected to a second deferred shock of puberty and is forced, either as an emergency measure or more surreptitiously, to make changes to his or her psychic economy in order to cope as well as possible with this new conflict and the structural modifications it entails.

To try to identify the initial—or initiatory—moment that triggers the parental crisis, we would in general study circumstances, perceptions, intuitions, verbal confrontations, and furtive looks; in so doing, we more or less invariably come across two complementary sets of affects and representations that involve, on the one hand, loss of the object and, on the other, reactivation of desexualized traces.

Perception of the young girl's transformations at puberty and the concomitant emergence of a young woman, imply the loss of the child she once was, the loss of an object that carried object-related and narcissistic cathexis. It is true that nobody has died, but some work of mourning will have to be done all the same; for example, for the loss of the various projections into the girl when she was still a child. As an adolescent, whether she likes it or not, she becomes a new object, and the new cathexis do not necessarily or easily replace the earlier cathexis on a simple one-to-one basis. Magical repetitions and imaginary identifications are turned on their head, as is the sense of "belonging".

Saying "my child" meant that everything was possible, including fantasies of bisexuality or of sexual neutrality; "my daughter" was more oriented, while "your daughter" was much more indicative of the state of the relations between the parents, affectionate or contentious; at any rate, the series of possessive pronouns had to stop short of the unutterable "my woman". Formulae, such as "you'll always be my little child", "child-like woman", "my child, my sister", and so forth, may be an attempt to tone down the shock, but they are above all an indication of denial and of nostalgia for an idealized era, that of the supposedly-neutral green pastures of childlike love; what has been lost is this retrospectively idealized period, together with the ideal child. Pride at being able to exhibit a beautiful brand-new object does not always compensate for the loss of the child who carried their desire for omnipotence and for everlasting narcissistic completeness.

The second set of representations and affects, often just as unconscious as the experience of losing an idealized object, is characterized essentially by the re-sexualization of traces that up till then had remained in latency. The girl's pubertal crisis reactivates not only oedipal desires in the parents but, more generally, a whole range of primal scene fantasies with their various associated conflict-ridden identifications. Together with the revival of oedipal and pregenital conflicts, a new economic structure of reawakened (or differently awakened) libido is set up: hence the need for a structural reworking, both quantitative and qualitative, of defence mechanisms.

To be more precise, I would like not so much to emphasize the classic oedipal rivalries and identifications, as to highlight what more insidiously unfolds, occasionally in a dramatic and painful manner, and directly or indirectly involves issues to do with fantasies of femininity and passivity. In line with discussions of feminine sexuality, phallic organization and the castration complex in both sexes (Cournut-Janin, 1998), we can see immediately that the confrontation with femininity, which the adolescent crisis in girls triggers, is not negotiated in the same way by the father and by the mother. "If she doesn't come back home, I'll kill myself," said the mother of the girl who ran away from home: this obviously implies that, *a contrario*, the departure of the daughter reveals the fact that she had become the object of new cathexis on the part of her mother. The daughter's running away meant, above all, for the mother a loss of love: she's going somewhere else, she prefers someone else. The "someone else", however, is not the father—who indeed also feels at a loss, helpless, and perhaps even castrated. The daughter's departure implies the loss of an object of narcissistic identification: she's "sleeping with" someone else, letting herself be penetrated passively, in other words, raped; if the virgin girl protected her mother against this possibly intolerable kind of femininity, the girl–henceforth-a-woman can no longer offer the same protection. In this scenario, there are also feelings of direct guilt (it's my fault) and indirect guilt through identification (it's her fault, but I am her and she is me), as well as shame: by disappearing, the girl, object of phallic cathexis, reveals the mother's castration fantasy. We know of course that the mother's phallic organization is often fragile; given the inability both to sacrifice *pars pro toto* and to hold on to the father's penis (he too is having a hard time of it), she has to fall back on her own paternal figure with all its failures dating from the time when she herself was an adolescent. At best, the mother will experience a nostalgic kind of neglect; at worst, she will collapse into a depressive state that brings in its wake thoughts of self-destructive acting-out. These acts will be all the more self-destructive if the disorganization of the phallic system and the disappearance of the family phalluses confront her with the *imago* of a primitive maternal figure who will intensify her feelings of guilt and shame.

Fathers of adolescent girls tend to focus on the look in the eyes: in their own, when they notice for the first time that their daughter is now a woman, but more particularly the glances they see in other men's eyes when *they* look at her. It is when they perceive the possibility of sexual desire in another man's glance that the femininity of their daughter is revealed to them—accompanied, again, by fantasies of rape and prostitution.

> "Your studies? Don't give me that rubbish! All you want is to get laid and play the whore!". After repeating this quote from her father, Myriam said she did not know for how much longer she could stand it. "He tells me so often that I'll end up walking the streets that one day it's almost bound to happen ...".

Giving in to the father's desire in order to keep him.

Whether this is a projection of an unconscious wish or the revealing perception of the possibility of such a wish, the father is obviously caught in the trap of a forbidden desire. If he gives free rein to his feelings of jealousy, we can sense the awakening of an oedipal desire—the desire to possess his daughter, as once he desired to possess his mother. In parallel with this desire, however, there is another one: the wish to be *like* his mother, passively receiving a man's penis, is reactivated behind the barrier of repression or the avatars of denial. The little boy the father once was knows well enough the "condition" under which that desire can be satisfied: being castrated, like his mother. Hence this situation, in fact, reawakens castration anxiety in the adolescent girl's father; the revival threatens to overwhelm the hard-won balance between his instinctual drives, especially now that his daughter, henceforth a young woman, will no longer play the part of a narcissistic phallic object that, in the psychic economy of the family, kept in check, for so long, the consequences of their fear of femininity.

In my view, fantasies concerning their baby daughter contribute to the fact that the parents tend to cover up the girl's vagina with a "phallic veil", as though the fond way in which the mother looks at the genitals of the man she loves were carried through into a cathexis of her baby: in this sense, both father *and* mother can see the child—a girl identified as such—as phallic and not as "pierced", thereby avoiding revival of the father's castration anxiety. The simple equivalence between penis and child also has the advantage of causing the third component to be "forgotten"; I am referring of course to the faeces, which bring anus and vagina too close together.

Given enough time (and as long as the father's capacity for integration is sufficient), this cathexis of the child as a narcissistic and phallic representation can enable a narcissistically frustrating movement towards gradual emergence of a relationship with the daughter as evoking his wife or his mother. Heterosexual cathexis and satisfaction, allied to an appropriate dose of sublimated homosexuality, may allow the father to "give"—to give away— his daughter to another man with whom, in fantasy, he creates or regains certain connections.

However, if these conditions are not met in the father's mind, the brutal risk of identifying with a desirable girl will trigger a whole series of defences, structured naturally enough along the regression–fixation axis, combining the withdrawal from feminine identification and the need not to lose the object. No longer a phallic object, the daughter may be recovered as an object cathected pregenitally, and, in particular, anally. This is when we encounter the strict supervision and control of her comings and goings, which globally restructure cathexis in a way that the father can feel comfortable with: controlled and supervised, his daughter is not lost, and at the same time the problem of castration is avoided. (As Marie put it, "My father's less of a pain in the arse ...").

Sometimes this will suffice, as though the phase of anal regression, in maintaining the relationship with the object, allowed for some working through of how cathexis are mobilized. In other cases, this libidinally-limited regression is overrun: it is an anal object, towards which highly destructive drive impulses are directed, that is henceforth manipulated and rejected. "If she doesn't come back home, I'll kill her". Lost as a phallic object and as a submissive part-object/stool, the girl is literally denied in her troublemaking existence with respect to the difficulties her father has to contend with in his mind.

Henceforth, the issue is one of castration–defecation, with the outburst of insults connecting together a destructive kind of orality and anality.

"For me, she's just a piece of shit". That was said of Fatima, who had had sex but had kept quiet about it for a long time before the secret was discovered; in a headlong rush to put an end to the problem, she committed suicide. The menfolk of the family declared: "She's better off dead", thereby unveiling the torrent of sadism to which her death finally put an end.

In, admittedly extreme, cases like these, where the masculine mind-set is given such a rough time that, in the wink of an eye, it suddenly sees the reflection of an unacceptable passive desire, this kind of deadly regression is probably caused by re-sexualization of the superego.

In discussing the sexuality of the girl-who-is-developing-into-an-adult, I have preferred to emphasize what may happen when the parents fail to process adequately in their minds the new situation with which they are faced.

As regards the father, the possibility of anal regression comes up against the problem of *pars pro toto*; the girl-part is sacrificed when this regression goes beyond mere control and can no longer maintain the libidinal relationship with the object.

As for the mother, the revelation of her daughter's vagina—if we put oedipal rivalry to one side for the moment—may revive primitive anxieties to do with her own father's penis, as well as with that of her husband. Whereas the father expresses his anxiety via anal–sadistic regression, the mother's own primitive drives with respect to the penis are reactivated in a manner she feels to be terrifying; guilt then forces her to suppress the *corpus delicti*—herself, guilty of revealing the vagina through the intermediary of her daughter in such an intolerable way. Henceforth, everything collapses into an all-or-nothing state of mind on the model of depression, as if all *she* could do was to take back inside her womb the bad object that her daughter has become for the father.

Summary

In these extreme cases, femininity seems to be unacceptable for both sexes, triggering a process that will destroy the object (or the object and the self, depending on the sex of the parent involved).

The model of castration enables the father, via projection and a regressive movement that protects the ego, to repudiate his daughter in a sacrificial way. The core problem involves the sacrifice of *pars pro toto*. "If she doesn't come back home, I'll kill her".

In the case of the mother, on the other hand, the lost object returns, much as in melancholia, and is reintegrated in order to destroy everything. The core problem here is that of all-or-nothing. "If she doesn't came back home, I'll kill myself".

For each of the three protagonists in this eternal affair—father, mother, daughter—faced with the horror of femininity, with its physical dimension and the glances that this attracts, the paternal cry of "Let's get out of here" is more often than not the expression of phallic overstatement—in the best of cases.

Notes

1. An earlier version of this chapter was published (in French) in *Psychiatrie de l'Enfant, Volume 2,* 1998. © PUF.
2. The "Point-Jeunes Paris". After five years, the city authorities closed down the Centre claiming that it cost too much to run ...

CHAPTER THREE

"Too late": ambivalence about motherhood, choice, and time

Nancy J. Chodorow[1]

T his paper investigates what we might call the non-reproduction of mothering (Chodorow, 1978, 1999b) or the disruption of generativity (Erikson, 1950). I suggest that in our time, as gender roles and family patterns change and as the culture interpreting biology and aging and the actual biological constraints of age shift, for some women internal conflicts and fantasies about having children or being a mother can meet up with these external changes to create painful crises, in which the wish to have children gets psychologically disentangled when it is simply too late. I describe how, culturally and psychologically, apparently non-gendered experiences of time intertwine with these gendered cultural and psychological phenomena in leading these women to put off or undermine their potential for motherhood.

The paper both challenges and confirms some of my previous work. Specifically, a historically—and still, in many ways— appropriate 1970s feminist psychoanalysis that challenged the existence of a single culturally and psychoanalytically normative path to femininity, including motherhood (Chodorow, 1978), might not sufficiently have taken into account the universal psychological necessity of interpreting and experiencing one's reproductive biology, as well as not recognizing potential difficulties in reconciling support for more options for women and the existence of multiple possible psychological trajectories with the equally necessary recognition of many women's internally felt drivenness to mother (see Chodorow, 1999b). The paper confirms my more recent suggestion (1999a) that projective and introjective filterings of culture, personally individualized dynamic interpretations and fantasies about embodiment, an individually constructed inner object world of self and parents, and affective constellations and fantasies that do not seem directly related to subjective gender (here, the relation to time), all enter into individualized animations of gender.

In the last half century, we have seen remarkable changes in the family and work lives of more privileged women. Numbers of women and men choose not to have children, and the age at first birth for women has increased. Professional women, especially, often our patients and colleagues, do not have children until their mid- thirties, forties, and even, occasionally, their early fifties. For many individuals, and even for "society", "the family" seems to have moved from a necessity to an option. In the United States, articles argue that workplaces discriminate against non-parents when they give pregnancy leave, allow part-time work, or enable mothers to leave work on time. The implicit attitude seems to be not that all of us need children to be born and well cared for; instead, having children is a personal preference of some indulgent individuals who should not be coddled. And although "the family" is not an option from the point of view of children, in the United States, at least, policies from welfare regulations to pregnancy-leave benefits and workplace requirements seem to assume that children do not need mothering—that somehow a caretaker or caretakers will be found.

Most of us favour these changes that have enabled women to engage in fulfilling and remunerative work (many of us *are* those women), and, as the question of "choice"—family life as an option—also comes up around women's right to abortion, most of us are firmly in favour of this right. Because of such beliefs, it may be hard for us to recognize some of the potential psychic concomitants of the general growth of "choice", not just the choice to keep or not keep a pregnancy, but of our current cultural belief—

one that I certainly share—that, for the individual woman, having children should be a choice rather than an assumed destiny. These concomitants are more likely to arise today than formerly, when it was simply assumed that most women would marry and have children, so that it required as much passive role acceptance as active psychological capabilities to achieve these ends.

Although classical psychoanalysis made pregnancy and mother-hood lesser features of women's development than genital experience and difference, these experiences are, from the beginning, central to women's psychosexual, self, and object-relational development, as well as constituting adult developmental phases or psychosocial crises (see Balsam, 1996; Bassin, et al., 1994; Benedek, 1956, 1959, 1960; Bibring, 1959; Bibring et al., 1961; Chodorow, 1978; De Marneffe, n.d., Kestenberg, 1956, 1976; Langer, 1953; Notman & Lester, 1988; Pines, 1993; Raphael-Leff, 1993). Motherhood begins, internally, in the conflictual, intense cauldron of childhood sexuality and object relations and is overdetermined, filled with fantasy, and complex: any women's desire for children, whether immediately fulfilled, fulfilled belatedly, or never fulfilled, contains layers of affect and meaning. Having children, just as not having children, can be freely chosen or pathologically driven, mired in conflict or relatively conflict-free. With either choice, each of which can have multiple meanings, we hope for a certain amount of secondary autonomy—a predominance of elements that have come to be independent of these originary conflicts. But if motherhood were not filled with so many different meanings and motives, we would not expect a mother to have a maternal identity and the special sense of herself in relation to her children that allows her to mother.

However, just as with all developmental theories (for example, we now distinguish erotism and object choice as developmental necessities from normative heterosexuality), we need to be careful to distinguish the inevitable internal working with or through the developmental challenge of reproduction from any assumption of a normative psychological or behavioural outcome. Thus, in con-sidering the non-reproduction of mothering, I am not suggesting that it is all women's destiny to bear or raise children, nor that it is more pathological to choose not to be a mother. Moreover, that all women (and men) give fantasy and dynamic meaning to their reproductive selves, bodies, and object-relations and that there are prevalent developmental patterns within this, does not preclude potentially infinite individual variation in these meanings and patterns (see Chodorow, 1999a,b). The dynamic and relational constellation that I describe leading to too-lateness, for example, differs from that described by Bergmann (1985), who also found in a number of patients a culturally and psychologically generated delay of motherhood (one that I recognize in others of my patients, centred in a precociously sexualized dyadic relationship to the father and symbiotic relation to the mother). Finally, although motherhood is usually one central meaning of generativity for women, generativity for both sexes means more than parenting one's own biological children. It can involve many kinds of creative work or work that fosters the next generation or the environment.

Just as I have emphasized that I am not beginning from the position that motherhood is all women's natural destiny, or that the choice not to have children is by definition pathological or problematic, I also note that the "too-lateness" I am considering is about regretted delaying, which may or may not result in infertility. In those older women who find that it is too late, I am not suggesting that infertility—when this, rather than either relational status or menopause seems central—is a sign of continued internal conflict about pregnancy. Psychoanalysis has been more likely to investigate infertility than delay (for an exception, see Bergmann, 1985), and although psychoanalysts can still fruitfully explore and treat cases of psychogenic sterility and infertility (Leuzinger-Bohleber, 2001; Pines, 1993), I agree with Apfel and Keylor (2002, p. 100) that "it is time to retire the term 'psychogenic infertility'" as having done more psychic harm than good for women (Apfel & Keylor, p. 85, also point out that "assisted reproductive technologies offer a more direct route to parenthood" than analysis). I am treating my patients' current wishes to have, or to have had, children, at face value.

In the patients I am considering, a variety of culturally supported beliefs have provided conscious rationalizations for attitudes to motherhood. First, they agree with a widespread notion—which certainly, in the United States at least, has much external reality to support it—that motherhood and professional life are incompatible for women, that the demands of modern professions for total commitment and a sixty-hour work week

assume a wife–mother in the home or two high-powered profes-
sionals without children. For many women, supported by some
strands of feminist ideology, the cost–benefit analysis goes one way:
what are the costs to a high-powered career of motherhood, rather
than the costs to motherhood of a career? On a more personal level,
these patients report observing their mothers' entrapment, passivity, suffering, and subservience to their fathers, as well as their
mothers' inability—from the daughter's point of view "because of
the children"—to assert themselves or leave their marriage.
Generated among some young women, from this observation of
trapped mothers and from feminist ideology, is an insistence (for
which, I ruefully find, some of my own early work provides fuel)
that they won't have children unless their partner promises to do
half the caretaking. If we are lucky, women come to us early enough
that we can examine the function of such beliefs in keeping deeper
fears of motherhood and pregnancy from surfacing, so that a real
choice can be made, but in women for whom it is "too late", this is
not possible.

Motherhood is, in conscious and unconscious fantasy, first and
foremost a gendered bodily, object-relational, and cultural experience for women, but gender, here as elsewhere, also gains personal
meaning and is constructed from non-ostensibly gendered phenomena (see Chodorow, 1999a). In the patients I am considering, this
non-gendered phenomenon involves a relation to time that itself has
implicitly cultural, as well as psychological, underpinnings. Many
cultural commentators have noted the late twentieth-century's cult
of youthfulness and the flight from aging; indeed, these trends have
been supported by astounding changes in longevity and health. As
people change careers in their fifties, as men remarry in their sixties
and father children, as fertility treatments allow women to get
pregnant in their forties and fifties, we can come to be fooled by
time. For women, these biocultural changes can contribute to the
fantasy that there is no biological clock.

The relation of time, change, and gender is also intrapsychic.
Building on Nietzsche, the psychoanalytic cultural critic Norman O.
Brown (1959) theorized that the denial of death and fantasies of
immortality generate morbid neurotic transformations, a deadened
culture, and a constant striving for change, rather than the capacity
to live life fully in the present. In a more clinical vein, several

analysts have explored the contradiction between, on the one hand, the necessary slow unfolding of an analysis, taking the analytic dyad out of ordinary time and recognizing the timelessness of the unconscious, and on the other, the necessity of acknowledging that time is in fact passing as an analysis progresses, that aging, life lived in the present, and mortality are really before us as we work (Buechler, 1999; Cooper, 2000; Hoffman, 1998). In a particularly beautiful paper, Arlow (1984) describes how variations in the sense of time and timelessness can, in some instances, access moments of eternity and in others, lead to a paralyzing inability to make any life choices—from writing down an appointment in an appointment calendar to applying to college or planning a family—that imply a future to be planned for or years to be counted. In women for whom it is too late, I also discovered that, quite apart from their current recognition of this too-lateness, time has in unconscious fantasy stood still. Analyzing this unconscious attitude toward time, then, becomes a primary route into understanding the psychology of the non-reproduction of mothering.

With these patients, we have both had to face the painful recognition that they would not bear children when they now very much want to and to recognize also how this not having children was due to their own conflicts and the behaviour that these conflicts generated. Our role as analysts is to mitigate psychological suffering and to promote self-understanding and self-acceptance, yet we are drawn to case reports with external fairy-tale endings: "when we terminated, Mrs A. was enjoying her work, sexually responsive to her husband, and pregnant". In one important respect, an external fairy-tale ending is not possible for the women who concern me, as we recognize the biological clock and the ending of possibility, but my experience has been that it is particularly difficult for these women to mitigate their guilt and self-blame. The challenge, then, is to help someone to get beyond feeling that her lack of motherhood is her fault and that she has damaged not only herself, but others in the process. For the analyst, perhaps particularly if the analyst is a woman whose maternal identity is powerful and who really does feel, deeply and profoundly, that there is no substitute (I refer to myself), there are also strong counter-transference feelings: it is hard not to agree with the patient that, on some level, there is something absolute and irretrievable in her situation.

Thus, I am thinking here not only of women who have used various feminist- or career-derived reasons for delaying motherhood and then find themselves up against the fertility clock, but of women who have more actively sabotaged their fertility and for whom time (hence, "too late") plays a particularly potent role in their psychology and the progress of their treatment. Several of my patients have had multiple abortions and/or been risk-taking sexually—since their teens having multiple partners, not protecting themselves, and/or not attending to uterine or vaginal symptoms. One case of very early menopause must certainly have been an unfortunate biological anomaly, but the patient herself attributed it to rage at her mother and at herself—to wanting to destroy her own uterus. These women may also more generally avoid or inhibit generativity, choosing jobs that masochistically punish and traumatize rather than fulfil, sometimes extremely demoralizing jobs that involve working with ravaged and destroyed people, or describing creative blocks. One patient in her early fifties describes sibling envy, rage at mother, and multiple abortions, but she has always consciously not wanted children. Yet she wrestled with a huge writing block, and she found it entrapping to keep a datebook and to write down changes of appointment.

For the woman I am considering, a kind of deadening anger has played a part. This is not a volatile or active rage, but rather an imploded, leaden, relentless self-destructiveness. The woman has deadened both self and object, in this case, the object including her own uterus. The affects and fantasies that have gone into disrupting this bodily and relational generativity seem to go to the earliest mother–child relation and to a core of deadening and deadened anger that has been turned both outward and against the self and the reproductive and sexual body. Especially, the origins of the anger seem to lie in the mother–child–sibling realm.

We are very much in Klein's territory here, specifically her description of early hatred of the mother and wish to destroy the mother's insides, but Klein's observation that fantasies of the mother's insides include other babies, as well as milk and the paternal penis, has not been, I think, enough attended to in our case reports. My patients feel there was not enough of mother, because there were several siblings, and because mother was depressed, downtrodden, submissive, and tired from taking care of so many children. They come to recognize a belief that they destroyed their mother with greed or envy, they elaborate on implacable envy of siblings or a memory of wishing to destroy them, and they report conscious memories of exaggerated adoring and protecting of siblings that, as we discover, veiled the wish to destroy them. Another way to understand the logic here is that the sib's desperate need for protection and adoration was because of the potential for destruction by the patient herself. There is, thus, ongoing anger at the mother and a fear of having destroyed, as well as a desire to destroy her, but siblings especially loom large. Moreover, I have not found the fear of maternal retaliation for destructive fantasies that Klein also describes: rather, the mother is already too tired and weakened—not just by the patient, but by her maternal life—to retaliate.

This developmental outcome was set in early childhood, but it runs up against, or alongside, a denial of time passing. Both treatment and life are more or less maintenance operations rather than progressions. The patient for some time does not believe that she deserves to improve, just to hold things steady and not be totally miserable. Patients talk about "keeping things timeless" and "running in place". Time forms a psychic retreat, represented not in spatial images of being in a castle, fortress, or otherwise walled off, but in talk about rolling back the clock or doing things over. Photos that capture particular childhood moments that resonate with conflicts with siblings and mother are fixed in the imagination as screen memories. And patients are continually surprised at their own age.

This sense of time standing still, progressing cyclically rather than linearly, proves a formidable resistance. First, it is not immediately noticeable (at least it was not for this analyst). It is a quiet resistance, a tacit assumption that manifests only indirectly, through the guise of the treatment not seeming to progress. Then, it is unremitting and relentless, since one of its functions is to deny the harm the patient believes she has done by rolling back the clock to before siblings became damaged or mothers died or became depressed and hopeless.

Kristeva (1979) claims that "women's time"—time from the unconscious point of view of motherhood and reproduction—is both cyclical and eternal. She is referring both to the cyclicity of the menstrual cycle and women's place in the cycle of generations and to the monumental, out-of-ordinary-time-and-space, tied to nature rather than culture, sense of pregnancy and involvement with a baby. This cyclical–eternal sense is to the time dimension what the oceanic feeling or primary oneness is to fusion in the dimension of space. It is—hopefully—part of the earliest experience and sedimenting of being, for the child and for the mother, who draws from her own experience of being mothered in relation to her child, and it is part of what many women bring to maternality and helps to constitute women's time (Arlow, 1984, describes a musician who feels penetrated by light and transformed during a Christmas Eve performance, feeling briefly a sense of being outside of time and part of eternity, merging with her music, her mother, her father, and an imagined Madonna pregnancy). Kristeva contrasts women's time with the linear and teleological time of history, society, and politics.

A distortion, or perversion (Chasseguet-Smirgel, 1985, describes the relations among creativity, perversion, and the recognition of reality), of woman's time, I think, figures into the timelessness or time standing still psychic phenomenon of these women for whom it is too late. Because of the rooting of the internal mother–child relation in early unconscious fantasies of destruction rather than generativity, the timelessness of the early mother–child bond, that a woman takes with her into her own reproduction of mothering, has acquired a deadened and imploded, rather than a emerging chrysalis quality. Cyclical time, rather than being active and in movement, becomes stopped or repetitively circular, and monu- mental, eternal time freezes. The psychological clock stops as age and time stand still, or time repeats and repeats, and the biological clock is also eliminated. To return to culture, my speculation is that this unconscious sense of time standing still is potential in any time and place, but it may be more likely in a culture like ours with its emphasis on youth, no aging, longer lives, later fertility, and a family life cycle that seems to have no fixed routine and to be a voluntary rather than a taken-for-granted option.

To make the clinical picture I have been elaborating more vivid, I describe in what follows two women, one of whom was largely unable to resolve her personal sense of too-lateness, and the other who was able to achieve such resolution.

J was in her early forties when she came to treatment. She had been living with the same man for four years and had hoped, she said, to have children with him, but she had not gotten pregnant. She was the oldest of five children, three spaced less than two years apart, followed by a gap of five years, then another closely spaced two. J reported from earliest childhood a total adoration and protectiveness of her two immediately younger siblings and tremendous guilt that their lives had been harder than hers, in a way that bespoke frantic keeping of her jealousy of them at bay. Her parents had been off-and-on separated for four years when an accidental pregnancy returned father to the home. Shortly after the last child was born, mother, again pregnant, had a miscarriage with severe haemorrhaging and was rushed off to the hospital for a hysterectomy, leaving J to take care of all her younger siblings. J was terrified that her mother would die, while also relieved that there would be no more babies, and she was confirmed in her perception of her father's rather brutal maltreatment of her mother and the family. To her relief, her parents shortly afterwards divorced.

J, who reported desperately wanting a family, described five abortions between the ages of twenty and thirty (five representing either the number of children that her mother would have had after her, but for the haemorrhaging and hysterectomy, or the five she had, including J herself).[2] As we reconstructed things, there had been a drivenness to these pregnancies, acquired either through brief one-night stands or with boyfriends whose even slight hesitation she used as a reason not to keep the pregnancy. J had gotten pregnant, it seemed, almost in order to have an abortion. J had decided in her mid-thirties that she wanted to have children and became involved with a man, but she chose a divorced man with a checkered paternal history, one who never saw his children. They began immediately trying to get pregnant, but with no success. When she was turning forty, J began to look into fertility treatments—began, because this looking was done with only a surface acknowledgement of her biological clock. J took time finding doctors, had trouble getting her boyfriend to join her for appointments, and wanted to tell neither him nor the doctors about her abortion history. Her several abortions were a constant source of self-punishment, a constant reminder that she had only herself to blame for ruining her chances to become a mother, as well as for destroying these potential babies. J was quite sure that through her abortions she had destroyed her capacity to get pregnant, and given her age and reproductive history, doctors were also hesitant about her chances.

Uncovering the self-attacking, in addition to the sibling-attacking, reasons for J's abortions was the work of long treatment. Before J began with me, she had been in analysis in another city for many years. She aborted that progressing treatment by finding a job that required her to move. During our work together, J often came late or had to leave early for meetings. Indeed, part of denying time was having three places to be, including with me, at literally the same time. J also occupied her hours with trivia from work, all, as she began to see, to keep feeling at bay.

As she reached her mid-forties, J had given up, recognizing that she would never be a biological mother: it became, in fact, too late. She had neither the resources, the stable relationship, nor, it seemed, the biological capacity, to become pregnant. We became more aware of time standing still or not existing, and that time needed not to exist, because recognizing that time moves forward would be to acknowledge the reality of too late. Fertility, getting pregnant, came to be understood as meaning not only or even mainly becoming a mother, but of making reparation and undoing the damage she had done to self, siblings, and mother. When J reached the too-late time, she felt that she could never undo this damage, never get over her sadness, guilt, and anger at the destructiveness she had engaged in. She had not protected, but had destroyed, her younger siblings, had wanted to destroy them, had destroyed her own potential children and her own reproductive capacities. J finally drifted out of treatment. When we discussed what it would mean to terminate rather than to end, to see her life as the life she has lived or that she might come to feel compassion for herself, J said that if this is what it would take, she could not finish treatment. She will always feel regret and will never accept what she has done with her life. Also, trying to accept herself would take time, and then she'd be even older. After the fact, J announced that she had begun looking into adopting, which seemed more in accord with her tendency to act to get away from feelings, but nonetheless also to resolve in some fashion at least the external outcome of her painful conflicts.

*   *   *

A second woman, S, for whom it was also too late, was able to resolve her internal feelings differently after a long analysis. Like J, S came from a similar, large family, in this case six children rather than five, of whom she was the youngest. S always felt that there was not enough to go around, that her siblings had taken everything from her mother already, so that her mother was now old, tired, and unable to give. Several of her siblings were successful, but, like J, S felt that her own destructive envy had been the cause of incapacity in those who were not. S had the same imploded anger at her mother for being unavailable and a relentlessly self-punitive sense that her mother's exhaustion was her fault: her own birth and feeding, specifically, had been responsible. S had exposed herself multiple times to sexually transmitted diseases through risky sex. She had not had abortions and in fact speculated that, given so much unprotected sex, she must have ruined her fertility. S also kept her analysis and life timeless, thinking of herself as a young girl or young woman, and not allowing our relationship to shift. Unlike J, for whom each friend's pregnancy was another painful blow, S simply did not notice that her friends were marrying and getting pregnant, or she noticed, but at the same time thought that she herself was not old enough to have children (I would also wonder whether the actual fact of pregnancy, getting pregnant, having or not having abortions and a more immediate reaction to the maternal uterus, might be more prevalent in older daughters of large families, who have watched their mothers' subsequent pregnancies, than in youngest daughters).

Investigation of the narcissistic cocoon of time standing still in the analysis, and of the need for time to stand still in order not to have had her destructiveness happen, freed S to accept that her non-fertility might be a result. In her late forties, she met a widower with two college-aged children—children of appropriate age for her to have been their biological mother. As she finished her analysis she was able to accept, without self-punitiveness, the life she had lived as hers, and she found herself engaging in generative nesting—remodelling a house, taking great pleasure in creating a beautiful flower garden, and learning how to relate to her new stepchildren. She said, "I have regret, but I can't change the choices I made. I'll never have children, and I have to go on with things. I can't redo my childhood, the things that happened, the choices I made. I can't undo my age, or my choices to be single for so long. There's no going back on it".

As our literature describes, it can be extremely painful and sad (for both patient and analyst) when a woman has trouble conceiving. In the "too late" cases of the non-reproduction of mothering that I am describing, this is made more painful by the woman's sense that she herself is at fault, not just for reasons of having put off getting pregnant or hormonal happenstance, but because of virulent anti-fertility forces within. This paper explores the (sometimes mutually constructed) defences and resistances that enter treatment around time and timelessness and the relation of particular family constellations to unconscious feelings about motherhood and a woman's reproductive body. I have suggested that these internal constellations, that lead to not having children, meet a shifting culture in which many facets conspire to make the delay of motherhood not noticeable. These include seeing motherhood as an active choice for women, a statistical rise in maternal age, and medical advances that enable prolonged fertility, foetal monitoring, and increased longevity. Such cultural tropes and trends can be further underpinned by feminist commitments. Finally, less visibly, but perhaps more insidiously, they include a meshing of woman's time with a culture that denies biological aging and implies that all things are possible.

Just as, when working with physically ill patients or patients dealing with bereavement, we can only work within the absolute reality of death, but cannot make death disappear, so, I think, we need to accept that there may be a sense of no possible substitute involved for women who very much want and cannot have children. I have suggested that what we can do, for women for whom it is "too late", is to help them to mitigate the virulent self-punishment and deadening of all creativity and generativity that can result, to accept their lives with integrity rather than despair. If we recognize the ways in which almost embodied unconscious fantasies of frozen time have fed into putting off motherhood and keeping treatment from moving forward, we can also be more attuned to look for manifestations of this particular psychic retreat earlier in treatment and, perhaps, to be able to analyze it before it is too late.

Notes

1. I am grateful to the Radcliffe Institute for Advanced Study at Harvard University for support during the writing of this paper.

2. Pines (1993, pp. 103–113) describes a similar patient whose "planned abortions" (p. 107) and inability to stay pregnant were symptoms of a deeper need to remain empty, dead and entangled with a destructively fused relationship with her mother.

CHAPTER FOUR

A "pause" for changing life: climacteric change and menopause

Gertraud Schlesinger-Kipp

I n the literature on women—also in the psychoanalytical literature—it is largely the case that the earlier three capital "K"s[1] have been replaced by four "M"s: menarche, menstruation, motherhood and menopause. I would like to raise these events in the life cycle to the status of facts of life, although they are frequently only mentioned in brackets.

Which facts of life are meant here and what is their significance in the psychoanalytical process? The theme of facts of life in life cycles of female development is—as you can imagine—full of traps: on one hand it is important that we are not talking in the following about the goal of a normative femaleness, which excludes all elements of the male or sees female development as a deficit variation of male development, as formerly was the case in psychoanalysis.

Women react to certain facts of life in their biography with different internal reality, which amalgamates both the physical, psychic, and social reality. The individual culture, naturally, also plays an essential role in the process. The influence of actual physical experience can be to instigate significant changes in the internal world. Likewise the internal representation of bodily changes in a life cycle can influence the perception of the reality of the body.

Even if it is no longer a matter of typical biographies—for nowadays women's biographies differ considerably—Erikson (1966) did for the first time set up a psychoanalytic basis for this individual perspective with his model of phase-specific developmental tasks. Our life is more, however—unlike that suggested in Erikson's phase model—than chronological time, more than numerical age; it contains likewise the "eon", the rhythmic, cyclical instinctive arc from birth to our conclusion, the time of contradictions.

After that there is, in different concepts of psychoanalytic biographical research, the following common ground:

1. there is psychic development not only in childhood and adolescence but also in adulthood;
2. childlike development refers, above all, to the building of a psychic structure. During development in adulthood there is a continued further development of this psychic structure and its "use";
3. the changes of the body and its images in the body scheme and the fact of mortality has decisive consequences on psychic development in adulthood;
4. there is the idea of relatively constant stable phases, between which there are transitional phases, "exchanges", in which determinate facts of life can create regressive crises; and
5. the handling of these crises in a biography is dependent on the solution of prior life crises.

Also, the development of sexual identity is by no means a singularly completed, defined structure, but must be achieved again and again. It is a question here of female self-images and not of femaleness versus manhood, a sexual identity which emphasizes in the course of the development the apparent contrast of the sexes, first of all in order to overcome them in the ideal case.

Theses on the psychodynamics of climacterium and menopause

There is a very old idea of the female life cycle: in the Demeter myth (according to Riedel, 1989) Persephone symbolizes Kore, the girl,

Demeter, the fruitful woman, and Hekate, the wise old lady, thus symbolizing the different life phases of women. Zeus—in agreement with the God of the underworld Hades—takes the girl Persephone, and then gives her to Hades in marriage. Demeter has a fit of rage over her daughter's kidnapping. In her despair and frenzy she makes the earth dry up and will not listen to any attempts at reconciliation. Only Hekate, the wise old woman and Demeter's mother, Rhea, have contact with her. As a last attempt at mediation, Zeus sends out the messenger Hermes, who like no other can reconcile differences and bring together male and female, upper- and underworld. He does not go first to Demeter, but to Hades, to convince him that Persephone must return, at least occasionally, to her mother, so that the world can become fruitful again. Hades seems to be reasonable and lets her go, but gives her a sweet pomegranate seed to eat. The pomegranate with its blood-red flesh and countless seeds is the fruit of Demeter in the ancient world, the possibility of fertility, which in Hades, the underworld, is the necessary requirement for life. Also, Hades needs a feminine half, to make things fruitful in the combination of underworld and upper- world, dreams and memories: the pomegranate seed in the hand of Hades stands for erotic–sexual pleasure and the bond connected with it. Persephone takes the fruit and discovers her erotic lust at the moment when Hades liberates her (as do so many women) Thus, after a time—in the ancient world always for a quarter of a year when on the earth nothing blossoms or flourishes, i.e. in winter—she will return to Hades.

Many mothers who experience this separation from their daughters and see their attention to a man as mischief, are seemingly angry, feel robbed, and like Demeter demand "temples" for themselves, desirous of reverence and obedience. This myth also symbolizes the change of the mother to unfertility while the daughter reaches the prime of life. The reunification of mother and daughter is not here to be taken as something real, but psychological. As I will go on to show, an internal reconciliation between mother and daughter is a possible achievement of menopause.

I must dispense with the grouping of the psychoanalytic literature concerning menopause here and can present only simplified theses which have emerged from this literature and my work with forty-five to sixty-year-olds, but also over sixty-year-old women. I refer here, predominantly, to the fact of life of "change" in menopause as a critical and crisis-producing time, the phase of middle age. However, in the same way, the years after sixty can also mean further emotional development and revision of old conflicts, thus demonstrating that people go to seek treatment for the clarification of lifelong conflicts. For many women, the psychic reality of later life means a renewed identity crisis centring around the early conflicts of fear, loss, helplessness, depression, narcissistic injury, and death. The difficult task of the integration of the aging body into psychic reality is introduced through the often furious internal disputes in menopause in opposition to the often sudden emergence of age in older men.

Since in my experience psychoanalysis is necessary and sensible not only in menopause but also after it, I will subsequently venture some remarks on transference and counter-transference problems that can result from the fact of life of age and the respective relationship to the age of the psychoanalyst.

Renewed liberation from the mother

Many women identify with the child in pregnancy and birth, and experience the situation with their own mother again. They experience fulfilment in pregnancy and the early mother–child phase that can be understood as a satisfaction of instinct and a happy symbiotic experience. Other women feel strongly threatened by the fact of childbirth and the concomitant symbiotic experience. This triggers excessive fear on the part of the mother of being devoured by the baby, expressing itself often in panicky fear for the baby or in depression. For the latter women, climacterium can lead to relief and psychic stabilization; however, most women will mourn the loss of these intense symbiotic experiences. It is important to point out that this need not be a case of an actual pregnancy or child, but can also revolve around imagining it, because the woman can still conceive.

Pregnancy means that:

> a woman no longer exists as a single individual, and an irrevocable
> mother–child relationship begins. One of the inner psychic tasks
> which a young pregnant woman has to master is the acceptance of

what one could call her "picture of her sex partner"—both in the
psychic and in the physical sense. That necessitates a fusion of more
recent libido and aggressive feelings with others, which are
anchored already through childhood experience—particularly
through the relationship to their parents and siblings and to their
own body. [Pines, 1993, p. 67]

In the course of a pregnancy, the body image of the pregnant
woman changes until she feels she is whole again and not emptied
out. However, at the same time, she must fuse with the child that
was once such an integral part of her body. After life "in the
mother's body" comes the first year "on top of the mother's body"
(Poluda-Korte, 1993, p. 84).

The end of the woman's possibility of pregnancy means a new
need to separate from her mother. It affects internal and often
external reality as well. In the internal reality a time of mourning
would be expectable, since the fusion of mother and child is no
longer possible—on whatever side of the symbiosis. After the
mourning—if it does not lead to depression—women often
experience a feeling of liberation, a strengthened identity. In
external reality, during this time, the actual loss is often also
experienced in the mother's death.

Sexuality and symbiotic wishes

Women in menopause often experience stronger sexual desire. The
discontent indicated in studies on sexuality often turns out to be
discontent with a partner, for as we know old couples are often
gradually less sexually active, and men also have age-related sexual
problems. So one can also understand many physical symptoms of
aging as signs of unsatisfied sexuality.

Intensified sexual experiential ability in menopause can, among
other possibilities, be understood as follows, since the elimination of
the fear of undesirable pregnancies is no longer a sufficient
explanation now in the age of contraception: the imagination of
the symbiosis that men experience predominantly in the sexual act
has its regressive counterpart in women's wish for children. This
possibility disappears in menopause and can be sought by women
and men alike in sexual symbiosis. For many women, sexuality is
still unconsciously connected with procreation. That can prevent

them from inwardly enjoying these rather male feelings toward sexuality.

Following Julia Kristeva (1994), one can understand the threat to the sexuality of women through the fact that they can no longer conceive. Also, in her dispute with Helene Deutsch and her notion of depression in women, Kristeva says about female sexuality:

> A woman encloses an inaccessible object within her body. "Phantasmatically and in the final instance this Inside is the Vagina ... the object concerned is a bad mother, whom a woman holds prisoner in order not to lose her, to master her, possibly even to condemn her to death. ... Two forms of lust seem to be possible for a woman in sexual relationships. On one hand the phallic lust—a contest or identification with the symbolic force of a partner, which mobilizes the clitoris. On the other hand a *different lust*, which ... is more directed to psychic space, but also to the space of the body. This other lust demands that the melancholy object which encloses the psychic and physical inside be brought literally to a melting point." [1994]

This can happen, according to Kristeva, only through a partner who is held to be suitable "of being more than a mother" to dissolve the imprisoned mother and to make a woman a present of something her mother never was able to give her—a new life. "A man gives her pleasure by giving her a child and personally becomes the connecting line between the mother–child relationship and the symbolic force" (Kristeva, 1994, pp. 222–223, translation by G. S.).

Does that, therefore, mean that a man again signifies something "less than the mother" without the possibility of pregnancy for a depressive woman? The imprisoned mother could then again dominate the inner body, as will become clear in the following idea of destroyed inner space.

The inner space

In the years of their fertility, every month women feel the pull between two poles, ovulation and menstruation. Ovulation entails the possibility of conception, birth, and motherhood and its concomitant bondedness. Menstruation, on the other hand, is a symbol for the contrasts of self-purification of the body and impurity, of fertility and destructivity, of sexual force and powerlessness and, above all, of independence. Since the hormone situation in menopause resembles that of the premenstrual time, women in menopause can suffer more from the loss of the subsequent facilitation of menstruation when the unconscious conflicts are not solved.

A woman, on the contrary, to whom menstruation is more important, emphasizes her independence and avoids the repetition of the symbiosis with the mother, the lust in the symbiosis. She suffers instead from menstrual complaints, because she frequently wants, through the above mentioned taboo, not to accept any great sexual pleasure during menstruation and transforms it into cramps.

Most women, on the contrary, are not fixed throughout their life to one or the other pole, but assign in different life phases more significance to ovulation or menstruation. The most pleasant days, shortly after menstruation, when all possibilities are open again, are brief, and then the next round begins. In analyses with younger women one can observe these constantly recurring themes in connection with the cycle.

Through the absence of menstruation in menopause, this fight between motherhood and independence disappears, but so does the possibility of the intense experience that cyclicity unconsciously provides.

The possibility of bearing a child gives women the secure feeling of having a good, healthy inner space. Without this security women can't defend themselves against developing notions of having a bad empty inner space (involved in, for example, a deep fear of cancer), which can lead to depressions.

The loss of the secure feeling of having a good fruitful inner space—an internal image of a good uterus[2]—leads only, via separation and mourning processes, to an integrated image of the body.

Moreover, older women often see their mother in their own body image. Depending on how much they are also able to allow the tender love towards the early body of the mother into the relationship with the aging one, they can accept their own body image inwardly.

Late revenge of the mother

Enraged and destructive phantasies regarding mothers are aggravated in puberty through feelings of rivalry and the idea of a possible victory over the mother, who is then usually in her climacteric change. According to Marie Langer (1953), climacterium and menopause can be experienced unconsciously as a late revenge of the mother for feelings of triumph during puberty. Feelings of guilt that cannot be compensated by a child can bring about depressions.

The phantasy of having survived the mother's revenge can also facilitate reconciliation with the mother. Daughter and mother in post-menopause are, so to speak, more "equal" than ever before. The oedipal rivalry can dissolve and a rapprochement between mother and daughter, without great feelings of guilt, is possible, since the unconscious guilt has been atoned for by the similar fate that befalls the daughter and the mother. In psychoanalytic treatment the mother can be approached without repeating the same fate.

Hypothesis: change in "daughterly existence"

The phantasy of being the ideal partner for the father who is younger than the mother and gives him a child again should be given up. When the incestuous wish is relinquished, mortality is accepted. Women must and can now at last give up their "daughterly existence" (Rohde-Dachser, 1990) and give up being the "self-object of the father" or, to put it in Freudian terminology, leave the "harbor of Oedipus", enticed by the new world to be discovered outside, on her own.

The relationship to the father and identification with him make it possible for a child to become independent of the mother early on.

A determining factor for the further development of a girl to womanhood is also the father's response to his daughter's femininity. Will he limit her oedipal victory over the mother and thus facilitate again and again her guilt-free return to the mother, without devaluating her own femininity? Will he shake her confidence as a woman by treating her as a substitute son? How can she successfully separate from her father in the course of her development? This is a question more seldom asked than the one regarding separation from the mother. However, it is a significant question in menopause as well, since fixation on "daughterly existence" entails the illusion of youthfulness and fertility. In phantasies and dreams these themes may continue to play a central role (and this is indeed the case, as dreams of my patients illustrate again and again), but the discrepancy with reality becomes larger, so that the danger of narcissistic wounds and depression grows. In order to feel well inside herself,[3] there also must be renewal and change in the oedipal relationship to the father. For some women, men thereby become so similar to the father of pre-puberty that they can no longer give them a child, and so they are flooded by incestuous anxieties.

Perhaps Freud's old question threatens to become virulent again in this crisis, however, namely that of how girls can successfully separate from their mothers, how they are to learn to give up the deep erotic bond to their mothers and get closer to their fathers. McDougall (1996), for example, leaves no doubt that women can integrate their original homoerotic feelings in the process of increasing motherly feelings towards children. However, if the intense time of mothering small children is past, and a man can no longer give her a child, the departure from the heterosexual solution to the oedipal conflict is again more probable and a strengthening of homosexual tendencies is to be expected.

The necessary internal restructuring for all these changes takes time. This time can be supplied, to some extent, by menopause: frequent hormone changes facilitate, as it were, a gradually better approach to post-menopause. The climacterium is also a chance to provide inwardly necessary separation work regarding changes in the activity of phantasy.

On transference, counter-transference and the fact of aging

Frequently, analysts are younger than their often middle-aged or older patients, a relationship naturally in constant evolution in the course of the analyst's own aging process and therefore requiring constant new reflection.

Does the question of the sex-specific difference in the area of the younger generation of analysts become more acute because, in addition to the classic transference/counter-transference relationship, the role of the therapist as child substitute with the corresponding reactions of the therapists comes into play as well? This is a fact, that in psychoanalysis with older people, is generally termed "multigenerational transfer" or "reverse transference constellation". It may be the case that male analysts often feel they are in the role of the son when treating older female patients and suddenly feel more like women often do: bonded, subject to power, inseparable from an omnipotent figure, threatened by diffusion, questioned as regards their competence, therefore suddenly in an emotional state that is otherwise rare in their function as analysts for younger patients. It is to be expected that they experience these feelings, among other things, as narcissistic injury. If they learn in their training not to be sexually attracted by their patients, but to deal with romantic oedipal feelings and to work with them, it is important here not to get into an early infant-like diffuse, dependent, and regressive love towards a mother and, on the other hand, not to have to defend themselves with the usual disqualifying tendencies towards women, particularly older women.

Furthermore, is it the case that female analysts have trouble working with older male patients because both their psychosocial, sex-specific expectations, and that of their patients, to be cured or cured by the love of a good daughter, trigger tremendous incestuous anxieties in the female analyst, anxieties more frightening than counter-transference feelings with younger male patients?

We must consider what a therapeutic relationship is like, in this context, between a female analyst and a patient who is about a generation older? As Pines, among others, describes, older female patients often very quickly develop an erotic transference towards the analyst. "Because there is not enough time, the patients are as it were liberated from the anxiety about humiliation and shame which had stopped them showing their feelings before" (1993, p. 165).

At the same time that the analyst in the daughter role triggers feelings of envy, the patient thinks that professional women, who grew up in the welfare state, essentially have more opportunities, whereas she feels robbed of her childhood or youth by National

Socialism, shocked by war experiences, and that she later had less career possibilities than women today.

The analyst, on the other hand, has the most experience in handling the regressive and homoerotic phantasies of female patients, likewise with negative transference and competition. In the role of the daughter, however, extremely confusing feelings are triggered: her fear of robbing the mother, of attracting her envy, as well as fear of growing old herself, and on the other hand, symbiotic desires of her own and the wish to be loved and cared for by the older woman.

If she, perhaps, feels such longings, she may develop greater problems in the final phase of treatment, since the patient's departure does not then mean something comparable to the children leaving the house, but the loss and death of a mother. The younger female analyst, on the other hand, has perhaps just liberated herself from her own dominant mother imago, and conquered the triangular world of psychoanalysis. Should she take such a risk? How can one talk to colleagues about it when even the actual death of one's own parents or their need for care is already a little discussed theme?

That is to say: one's own feelings in the role of the daughter dominate and are much more perturbing than the classic counter-transference feelings, so that it is correct to say that the problems of psychotherapy with older patients are mainly the problems of the analysts themselves.

Notes

1. In German: "Kinder, Küche, Kirche" i.e. "children, kitchen, church".
2. In German: "Gebärmutter" i.e. "birthgiving-mother".
3. In German: "zu Hause" i.e. "at home".

CHAPTER FIVE

Gender and affect[1]

Matilde Ureta de Caplansky

"I love this body that binds me.
The nipple erect on the sad chest.
The brief bitterness of its mouth.
The tender forlornness of its feet.
I love this body that traps me and *the mirror*
In which this body is reflected and becomes one.
The beautiful abyss of its sex.
Its sweet continence.
Its blue depth.
The wet clitoris that meditates.
I love this body that binds and condemns me"

Doris Moromisato (To this body in love), 1988, p. 25

"I look at my sex with tenderness
My pure gland and my testicles
Filled with bitterness
I am not the one who suffers but the other
The same millenary ape
Reflected in the mirror who weeps"

Jorge Eduardo (Eielson), 1955, p. 221

Introduction

I n this paper I assume that Freudian bisexuality and the "pure" female and male elements, in the Winnicott sense, *exist in both sexes.*

As hominids, all of us, both men and women, experience the same affects. However, there are gender-related differences in the way we express them, as we will see later. How can we explain these differences? How are they expressed?

Today, we clearly distinguish the concepts of man and woman as organisms that are biologically and functionally different; there is also a clear difference between the concepts of masculinity and femininity, as constructions—cultural constructions—that have gradually been shaped and formed from the earliest years of life. This is what we call gender.

Gender, according to our current knowledge, is a dimension which, as a reference, appears prior to the awareness of the anatomical (bodily) differences between the two sexes (Freud, 1925).

Also, gender organizes "adaptation", understood as:

> ... the consolidation of an autonomous self, the relationship between the self and the other, the search for meaning and the need to accept one's place in the cycle of generations, including the fact of one's own mortality ... [Spector Person, 1994, p. 64]

These are universal problems for both men and women, and although the solutions put forward in response to these questionings may vary, *the underlying dilemmas, as we may see, are the same.* The diversity of genders and sexual difference are disjunctive concepts whose manner of relating is complex and not unidirectional. It implies a coexistence in tension (Glocer de Fiorini, 2001).

In this perspective, while the reflection I present here is part of the extensive and age-old debate on the difference between the sexes, at the same time it is circumscribed to my experience in psychoanalytic clinical practice at this moment in time and in my specific environment.

Based on a couple of key points, I will attempt to propose an approach—always incomplete and segmented—to "our working hypothesis": *namely, though the affect is sexless, it does possess gender.*

Some vignettes

Vignette I

Miguel is a forty-five-year-old economist, divorced, with one son. He is nice-looking, successful in his social life and work relations. His main complaint is expressed through the conflicts in his relationship with his partner.

He has been in analysis four times a week, for two years. The following material belongs to the second year of the process.

> *Miguel*: I spent five years stuck to her. The sensation is that I'm going to "dilute", that "she is depriving me of air, stifling me" and that's when I have to fight ...

> "If I let myself get wrapped up", Lali is very narcissistic. The world belongs to her, and everything begins with her ... I have to make my way up and do my things. All couples are the same, "women want to absorb men and *vice versa*"..."I get all distant" and when I go home to sleep "alone"... phew!, "a bit of air". I feel like "flying" ... but I know that after a time I feel bad, lonely, I miss her ... that's the point, that's my story.

This defensive type of stubbornness to communicate coexists with its opposite: the fusional relationship, where the individual communicates, both internally and secretly, with an integrally good object in order to bear the frustrations produced by the absences or conflicts generated when in contact with the object (Green, 1993, p. 397).

> *Analyst*: If I've understood right, will this mean that here, between the two of us, the story could be the same?

> *Miguel*: [silence] ...I don't feel it's like that here; rather the feeling of being listened to, "empathized with", loved, is more important for me here ... [silence] ... I don't know whether this sounds childish, but "this place is more like a meeting place, my couch, my analyst, my session ... the war is outside ...

Miguel has not yet established limits between himself and his image of the mother as a primary seductive object. Therefore, in order to defend himself from this image, he needs to set a definite, specific distance in his relationships, particularly in regard to certain types of demand of the object. (We would have to verify whether this occurs only in men).

Analyst: My couch, my analyst, my session ... the war is outside ... perhaps because you're not yet able to accept the fact that a war can be here as well as outside, that maybe the point is that whenever you have to get into a relationship with someone else you feel, as you said, that you "dilute" with the other person (fusion) and that makes you feel bad ...

Miguel: [silence] ... Yes, it could be ... though I never thought of it that way ...

I use the above material to illustrate the concepts of affect and gender. Let us first take a look at the affect which, as we know, is one of the components of the psychic representations of drive, and becomes conscious through discharge. This *"discharge"* is mostly directed *"toward the body"* (Green, 1975). Miguel's allusions are fairly obvious. He says: "... the feeling that I am going to dilute, that they are stifling me ... I let myself get wrapped up ...". We recall that in addition to the seat of the first affects, according to Green (1975, 1995), in the range of pleasure–displeasure, we find secondary affects, already nameable and more sharply outlined. Affect is therefore what circulates "between the lines" "like an unspeakable strip" of climate or atmosphere that accompanies the individual like a continuum, both on the surface of the body and in the individual's intersubjective relations (Green, 1975, 1995).

We would say that affect implies intra-subjectivity and intersubjectivity, in a sort of dialogue, with those who matter to us during the course of our life. And, in regard to that dialogue, scenes or *"psychic matrixes"* simultaneously become articulated, to the extent that we have certain experiences, at a specific level, that are essential experiences for men and women, namely: birth, breastfeeding, being weaned, sphincter control, upright posture, exploration as a predecessor of more extensive socialization, learning to speak, and making use of symbols. The human being arises from this sequence, since these experiences are universal and deeply mark both sexes.

Reference to the early years of the mother–infant relationship is important in psychoanalysis, since both genders are "at the mercy" of the maternal function or dysfunction. The fact that Freud should have called this stage the *"primordial femininity"* stage has, as I understand it, something to do with a "cultural–psychological" bias as to what femininity means, because "in the strict sense" this experience, as we just mentioned, relates to both sexes.

There is no denying the importance of this period, and it may well be that the difference in the way one feels and expresses oneself has something to do with the early experiences of that "absolute dependency". Perhaps it is at that time that the so-called "dramatic affective dissociation" of men[2] is produced, in the sense that being tender and expressing affects has the cultural connotation "of weakness and vulnerability", traits which the culture regards as belonging to the female gender.

In another session, Miguel says: "... if a woman I am interested in were to tell me I am tender, it would bother me ...", referring with a clear "macho demand" to the fear of phallic castration: not having an erection, not having the possibility of "penetration".

Other such testimonies from literature refer to this topic. We quote:

> Among us men we don't talk about love, as if the frailty of that sentiment belonged to weak beings. Neither do we speak about our many sexual difficulties, our atavistic fears, our bewilderment with impotence, our dissociation—so common—between love and sexuality ... [Barrio Tarnawiecki, 1993]

In this context, despite his apparently privileged position—I say "apparently" in reference to the above-mentioned aspects that link "affect" with phallic castration and inferiority—a man's situation is difficult and complex, as evidenced by many different testimonies. Men also face day-to-day situations in which affects, values, and hierarchies are at stake. Some of those mandates that culture has imposed on men are probably linked to the idea that being a man is equated to going through trials, facing challenges, having to belong to the male gender and lastly, having to assume the exhausting symbolic sentence dictated by culture, in terms of equating the male with power. Here, we are dealing with cultural mandates that imply "pathetic" efforts on the part of men to make it appear that the ideals of power and virility as synonyms have been attained.

If we recall that a man is brought into the world and raised by a woman, we understand that he is involved in the task of resignifying (après-coup effect) this fact for the rest of his life, convincing himself and others that he has escaped from two important issues: that he is neither a woman nor a baby nor a homosexual.

Stoller (1986) reports that the roots of what we call masculinity (concern with being strong, independent, hard, cruel, polygamist, misogynist, and perverse) are defences against the facts of having been brought into the world by a woman and having been a passive and defenceless baby. These considerations allow me to propose a parallel with the descriptions I have attempted to make.

Vignette II

Sofi, twenty-seven, is a dancer of modern dance and is single. She has been coming to sessions because she can't bear "her anguish and her sorrows". She is pretty and attractive. She has been in analysis four times a week for one year. The material I present here is extracted from the first few months of the process.

> *Sofi*: I've been feeling bad ... anguish ... my heart crushed in my chest. I had no desire to be with him. I tried to feel like it, but I didn't manage to. I was very angry. I realized this clearly when I had sex with him and I felt very frustrated ... he doesn't even know I exist ... he feels placidly happy, turns over and falls asleep ... and of course, according to his idea, I should feel the same too ... and that's not the way it is ... and I get furious ... frustrated ... I try to tell him but he looks at me and doesn't believe me, or else he stops speaking to me for three days ...

This is the typical discourse of a woman who feels she is an object and demands attention; at the same time, it is the complementary pole of Miguel's defence against the female demand.

> *Analyst*: I was wondering two things: how and what do you try to tell X (her fiancé), who looks and doesn't believe you and then doesn't speak to you for three days? And how do you relate that to the fact that you haven't seen each other for three days? Perhaps

you're telling me that you've felt lonely, frustrated, and abandoned here, and that this is making you very angry . . .

Sofi: It's both things, with him and with you [she cries bitterly, shifts her position on the couch, sits up, lies on her side in a foetal position] and, looking out of the corner of her eye at me, says "softly": Why do I get so upset? . . .

The woman's intolerance for separation: "the role of being there" establishes a difference with the male in analysis, in relation to the analyst: wanting to be close but not merged together.

Analyst: That's a good question . . .

Sofi: I know . . . I mean, I know the answer . . . at least, I know it intuitively . . . I don't want to be left alone, to be uncared-for, unattended . . .

This female discourse, so frequently heard in our offices, takes us back to Green's (1975) description of how the affect proposes scenes in the manner of psychic matrixes which, like silent, emerging elements, carry entire subsumed fragments of an underlying history. Freud himself said: "The affect is always right" (1900).

We see, above, that the affect is the result of a sensorial drive complex, deployed in the field of intersubjectivity, which constitutes a series of sensations, perceptions, circulations of energy, feelings, and eroticism which, in turn, gender will organize.[3] The resignification (*après-coup*) of experiences and processes structures the psyche and have, of course, their own affects.

Listening to Sofi, we reaffirm that something happens to the woman that is "different from what happens to men", after the initial moment of physical and affective fusion with the mother; in her process toward femininity, she will have to separate from her in the fantasy of completeness and fusion with her, to relate to the father, whom she will love for a time . . ., then, she will realize that he will never "be for her" either, won't be her husband or her son. Again she is up against an "uncertain fate", in which the weight of the conditioning facts in the biological, psychological, and cultural dimension will be enormous. The girl will then want, through an incessant displacement operation, narcissistic reassurance from the man, reassurance that will consist basically of confirmation of his love, and she will make that a central issue in her life; she will demand to be adored, and her permanent complaint (which reminds us of Freud's statement about the "female complaint", in "Analysis Terminable and Interminable", 1937) will be that she is not sufficiently loved, understood or supported.

In this context we try to find where to locate and how to understand the origin of the differences in affective expression. Culture has greatly influenced the comprehension and study of this theme,[4] so much so that it is impossible to speak of men and women and their affects in the abstract; we need to place them in a specific context, just as no individual exists without inscription in a culture and a genealogy.

Epilogue

In synthesis, I maintain that the affects have no sex but do have gender, since their form of expression varies.

I also maintain that the body is the privileged space for that affective expression where we can identify the bonds between men and women.

Finally, I propose that the experiences encountered during the stage of the so-called *"primordial femininity"* contain the key—in the psychic aspect—to the differences in expression of the affects: dissociation in the case of men and the eternal demand for company in the case of women.

We must add that the plot-line of each history repeats the same structuring occurrence, essentially bearing witness to the bisexual nature of each of them. We thus recognize the plurality of the conformation of the individual—who owes his or her origin to the process of identification in which not only culture as a whole but also "personal history" appears. Hence, every man and every woman shows, in his and her personal statement, a history with a twofold origin. As indicated by Pontalis (1982): "facing the allocation of a sexual identity, a lifetime is not too long for each and every one of us to personally respond to the answers that were already given".

Notes

1. This paper was presented at the 41st International Congress for Psychoanalysis-IPAC Chile. "Affect in Theory and Practice", July 1999. I wish to thank Doctors Raquel Zak de Goldstein and Mariam Alizade for their comments and their unfailing company during my task.
2. Personal communication of Dr Raquel Zak de Goldstein.
3. I will use the gender concept of Spector Person (1994): "... masculinity and femininity (somewhat different from the biological concepts of man and woman) are parallel constructions, not ordered by nature, but irreversibly modeled in the earliest years of life".
4. Dupré, a philosopher of the Stanford team, contends that it is false that there are intrinsic human traits that differ between men and women which explain human behaviour if one does not take into account the historic and cultural context.

CHAPTER SIX

The ambiguity of bisexuality in psychoanalysis[1]

Simona Argentieri Bondi

"We, on the other hand, standing on the ground of
bisexuality, had no difficulty in avoiding impoliteness"

Sigmund Freud, 1933

A s we all know, the revision of Freud's concept on
femininity has sparked off a vast and interminable debate
that continues to this day.

Exploration of the very early levels, as well as the orientations of
the various schools of psychoanalytic thought, have suggested
many approaches to the problem of the "differences" between male
and female: in the development process, in biological "destiny", in
the interplay between identification and disidentification, in the
vicissitudes of sexuality ... and this debate has always led to
enrichment on a much wider scale, because every debate on
femininity inevitably involves that on masculinity, within the fertile
relational dimension.

However, the price that we have to pay for this thematic
enrichment is an equally unavoidable amount of confusion between

theoretic models, terminology, and conceptual hypotheses that are often difficult to reconcile and integrate.

Although it may be true—as Wisdom says in his 1983 work "Man and woman"—that in order to settle the problem of male or female, it is not sufficient for the midwife at the time of the birth to attribute to the human offspring one or the other sex, it is equally true that our debates on the subject have by now become so sophisticated and tortuous that they sometimes resemble the sterile theosophical diatribes about the sex of the angels.

On this occasion, however, I do not intend to speak about the open divergences; but rather about an area of consensus—in my opinion only apparent—that often comes about during theoretical–clinical discussions on the subject of the investigation of the "feminine". There is, in fact, a *concept*—that of *bisexuality*—that tends to emerge at a critical moment in these debates, and that acts as temporary pacifier or balance between the opposing factions as they try to define the problem of the similarities and the differences, of the "more" and the "less", between men and women.

If "things don't add up", especially in clinical work, concerning the supposed requisites that the patient—but also the analyst—ought to have in relation to the model that is from time to time established for his or her own sex, by invoking the "male half" in the case of a woman, or the "female" half in the case of a man, the contradictions, "injustices", and resentments can seem to be placated under the aegis of universal bisexuality.

Moreover, what exactly is intended by bisexuality is almost never specified: whether it is an "all-powerful" condition of "natural" double male–female identity of each, or whether—far from being a double identity—bisexuality is the indication of a confused and indifferentiated primal situation.

History of the concept of bisexuality

From the historical point of view, it must be remembered that the concept of bisexuality did not originate with Freud. He himself openly recognizes this in "Psychopathology of Everyday Life" (1901, Chapter 7, p. 143) in which he writes:

One day in the summer of 1901 I remarked to a friend with whom I used at that time to have a lively exchange of scientific ideas: "These problems of the neuroses are only to be solved if we base ourselves wholly and completely on the assumption of the original bisexuality of the individual". To which he replied: "That's what I told you two and half years ago at Br. [Breslau] when we went for the evening walk. But you wouldn't hear of it then". It is painful to be requested in this way to surrender one's originality. I could not recall any such conversation or this pronouncement of my friend's. One of us must have been mistaken and on the "cui prodest" principle it must have been myself. Indeed, in the course of the next week I remembered the whole incident, which was just as my friend had tried to recall it to me; I even recollected the answer I had given him at that time: "I've not accepted that yet: I'm not inclined to go into the question". But since then I have grown a little more tolerant when, in reading medical literature, I come across one of the few ideas with which my name can be associated, and find that my name has not been mentioned.

In this elegant example of the particular memory disturbance that Freud subsequently called "cryptomnesia", there is no sign of all the tortuous contentions that characterized the attribution of the priority of the concept of bisexuality in human psychology. In the first edition, instead of "a friend" he wrote "my friend Fl."; and "Fl." obviously stood for Wilhelm Fliess. We know that the first violent argument between the two friends took place in the summer of 1900, but their correspondence continued for several more years.

The most unpleasant episode, however, occurred in 1903 when Otto Weininger's book *Sex and Character* (*Geschlecht und Character*) was published. In his excellent biography *"Freud"*, Peter Gay gives ample space to the question. The book had caused a certain amount of scandal, not so much for its content (a biological–philosophical pastiche, full of strange psychological lucubrations, misogyny, and anti-Judaism, mixed up with an occasional original intuition), but for the melodramatic suicide of its young author who, at the early age of 23, took his life in Vienna by shooting himself in the house of Beethoven.

Fliess read Weininger's book and with good reason was deeply disturbed because, as he wrote to Freud in 1904, it laid out his ideas on bisexuality and on the "consequent nature of the sexual attraction: effeminate men attract masculine women and *vice versa*" (our translation).

The doctor from Berlin is very attached to "his" idea, as if it were a kind of "personal copyright", comments Gay. He suspects, or rather accuses, Freud of making known his speculations or of speaking with Weininger either directly or through Hermann Swoboda, a patient of Freud's and friend of the author of *Sex and Character*. Freud's attempts to settle the argument, even by postponing the publication of the *Three Essays* until Fliess has published his work, are useless.

In 1906, Fliess finally published his pompous work, *Der Ablauf des Lebens* (*The Course of Life: the Foundations of an Exact Biology*) and at the same time A. R. Pfenning, publisher and librarian, accuses Swoboda and Weininger of plagiary and Freud of being the channel for this theft of ideas.

One could comment that this idea of the double male–female nature of every human being is in reality a general and universal phantasy, present in mythology ever since the origins of history, and in the unconsciousness of all humanity well before the existence not only of Fliess, but also of Freud and of psychoanalysis itself. But this brief historical introduction has, above all, given me the opportunity to say that, in my opinion, ever since it made its appearance in psychoanalysis the concept of bisexuality has caused nothing but trouble.

Returning onto conceptual ground, we may underline that, according to Fliess, human bisexuality has its foundations, not only in biology and anatomy (the nose with its protuberant form and cavities suffused with blood would be the dominant organ and the most explicit corporeal exponent of the duplicity of the "male and female genital places"),[2] but even in mathematics, according to precise biorhythmic cycles of 23 and 28 days by which the health and sicknesses of men and women would be worked out in a complicated interweaving of additions, subtractions, intervals, and multiplications of these "key numbers". Thus, Fliess pursued his own personal dream of a human right to perennial ambiguity, but under the scientistic protection of the absolute.

Freud, as we know, did not go as far as this; but for him, too, the concept of bisexuality must be seen as firmly rooted in the biological and anatomical heritage of both the sexes, and as proceeding from the embryonic hermaphrodite residuals towards a psychological identity structure of a "monosexual" nature, male or female: "The dominant sex ... has repressed the mental representation of the subordinated sex into the unconscious" (Freud, 1919, pp. 200–201).[3]

It is surprising that the fragility of the Freudian hypothesis of being able to find, in human psychology, the ontogenetic recapitulation of philogenesis—so often criticized in other contexts—has survived almost intact in the psychoanalytic debate about bisexuality. To my mind, the work of Freud in which the psychopathological importance surrounding the concept of bisexuality emerges most clearly is "Hysterical phantasies and their relationship to bisexuality". Here we read:

> The bisexual nature of hysterical symptoms, which can in any event be demonstrated in numerous cases, is an interesting confirmation of my view that the postulated existence of an innate bisexual disposition in man is especially clearly visible in the analysis of psychoneurotics. An exactly analogous state of affairs occurs in the same field when a person who is masturbating tries in his conscious phantasies to have the feelings both of the man and of the woman in the situation which he is picturing. Further counterparts are to be found in certain hysterical attacks in which the patient simultaneously plays both parts in the underlying sexual phantasy. In one case which I observed, for instance, the patient pressed her dress up against her body with one hand (in the role of the woman), while she tried to tear it off with the other (in the role of the man). This simultaneity of contradictory actions serves to a large extent to obscure the situation, which is otherwise so plastically portrayed in the attack, and it is thus well suited to conceal the unconscious phantasy that is at work. [...] In the treatment of such cases, moreover, one may observe how the patient avails himself, during the analysis of the one sexual meaning, of the convenient possibility of constantly switching his associations, as though on to an adjoining track, into the field of the contrary meaning. [1908, pp. 165–166]

We shall return to this Freudian interpretation of the body as "theatre" of bisexuality, and to the resistential possibility of switching the tension of the conflict onto the "adjoining track".

At this point in our discourse, we turn to one of his later works—the famous *Analysis Terminable and Interminable* (1937)—in which

Freud individuates in the "repudiation of femininity" the "bedrock" that cannot be probed with the tools of psychoanalysis.

> ... it is the source of outbreaks of severe depression in her, owing to an internal conviction that the analysis will be of no use [...] we often have the impression that with the wish for a penis and the masculine protest we have penetrated through all the psychological strata and have reached bedrock, and that thus our activities are at an end. This is probably true, since, for the physical field, the biological field does in fact play the part of the underlying bedrock. The repudiation of femininity can be nothing else than a biological fact, a part of the great riddle of sex [...] Something which both sexes have in common has been forced, by the difference between the sexes, into different forms of expression ... difference between the sexes. [p. 252]

And this "something", both for the man and for the woman, would be the refusal of femininity, in the guise of castration anxiety in the man and of penis envy in the woman.

Therefore, although, for Freud, repression is an entirely psychological modality, resistance has a biological foundation as does the bisexuality that prevents women from resigning themselves to their destiny of not being men, and men from freeing themselves from the eternal obscure threat of their "feminine part".

Hence, not only is *bisexuality always closely linked to drive* (and for Freud, drives are a "bridging" concept between body and mind); but precisely because it *is rooted in the biological* "bedrock" of human nature, it is by its nature *not analyzable* outside of processuality and development, and therefore, as Freud writes, "does not allow for any change".

"Bisexuality, like anatomy, is destiny".

After Freud

After Freud, the concept of bisexuality retains its right to citizenship in psychoanalytic thought; but it progressively loses its specificity, detaching itself both from biology and from drives, and assuming shades of meaning that become increasingly vague and ambiguous. For the sake of brevity, I shall quote the comments that Rycroft makes under the heading of bisexuality in his useful *Critical*

Dictionary of Psychoanalysis (1968), where he writes that this term rarely refers to a person who has both "hetero" and "homo" behaviour and sexual relations: more often, it refers to male and female psychological attributes and attitudes that are both present in the same individual.

In his opinion, bisexuality is to be led back onto mainly psychological ground, and is based on the fact that children of both sexes, as they grow, identify themselves with both their parents. He concludes that connotations and non-sexual functions can be attributed through the concept of bisexuality. For example, "passive submissive, masochistic, intuitive, receptive" behaviour can be designated as feminine, and the opposite behaviour—"active, affirmative, sadistic, intellectual, penetrative"—as masculine.

Under this brief item, Rycroft does not stop to analyse what is meant by "identification with father and mother", and he does not distinguish between the external aspects of the socio-anthropological variations and the internal psychological processes of identity structure and gender identity. Following our discourse, however, it is clear, as he correctly points out, that—*after Freud*—*the concept of bisexuality moves away from sexuality and drives to indicate functions, behaviour, and identifications.*

I think it is also worth briefly mentioning the fact that the subject of bisexuality is sometimes used even by those psychoanalysts in whose frames of theoretic reference this concept has no place.

In Lacanian thinking, for example, in view of the predominant importance of the symbolic value of the phallus, there is not much room for so-called bisexuality. The same applies to the Kleinian concept, although it does speak of a "feminine phase" common to the two sexes (an attitude towards the father as secondary object, in an attempt to overcome the painful ambivalence of the primary relationship with the mother); or else reference is made to the "compensatory solidarity", as a possibility for males to identify with women on the basis of love and interest for the inside of their bodies; or, again, it speaks of "combined parental figure" at the level of highly persecutory partial objects, as an image of the mother who contains the penis of the father.

In an article I wrote in 1982 entitled "Sui processi mentali precoci dell'identità femminile: il rifiuto della femminilità e l'invidia del pene" ("On the very early mental processes of feminine identity:

repudiation of femininity and 'penis envy' "), I made some other remarks about the impact of Melanie Klein's ideas on this subject in the development of our theory and above all in our clinical work.

We know that Melanie Klein, by "anticipating" her investigation from the "classical" Oedipal age to the first months of life, was able to attempt the analysis of very early thought processes; and by exploring and privileging the mother–child relationship, she has shown that the deeper the investigation into the developmental levels, the more the experience of males and females with the mother and her breast coincide and converge.

Certainly, Klein's conceptualization—as well as showing the "defensive" and secondary quality of penis envy, in sharp contrast with the concept of Freud and of the early analysts who considered it an obligatory vicissitude of the instinct—has the advantage of moving the accent from an anatomical–morphological formulation to a relational situation in which envy—just as inevitably—develops within the early mother–child relationship.

From both a theoretical and an operative viewpoint, if we are able to lead analysis away from the "unchangeable bedrock" of the biological, towards a phase, albeit obligatory, of the early vicissitudes of oral aggressivity, then we are back again in the field of analysability.

I wonder, however, whether this concept of breast-envy is not often used in a too generic and summary manner; for the tracing back of every future complication and oedipal differentiation to the primitive oral anxieties, can certainly undramatize the importance of penis-envy and can provide for a generic "pacification" and "equality" between male and female.

Although justice may have been rendered to many interpretative abuses of the past (intra- and extra-analytic), by uniting the vicissitudes and leading the nucleus of every future envy back to the breast, we also run the risk of flattening the specificity of developmental events. The object of this envy—whether penis or breast—is always understood as a concrete fact, without taking into account the dynamics, albeit potential, of the developmental levels of thought from the concrete to the abstract.

I think that, behind the envy, there is often the traumatic primitive experience of the child who feels himself as separated, and therefore fragile, defenceless and mutilated of a part of himself. This mutilation, to which so many of our patients (male and female!) refer when they tell us about their painful sensations of incompleteness, is experienced, I think, as a wound—and the earlier the traumatic moment, the more corporeal and concrete it is felt to be.

To this sensation of missing something, I think we can reductively give the name of penis-envy, but also breast-envy, in order to apparently re-balance the disadvantage between males and females; or we can call it nostalgia for lost bisexuality. But by doing so, in my opinion, we risk inducing iatrogenic interpretations that function as "organizers" in the patient's minds and allow them to appeal to the "destiny" of that of which they have "biologically" been deprived, rather than confronting, in the dimension of the analytic relationship, the elaboration of separation vicissitudes, with the relative development of the thought processes from the concrete "biological" level towards symbolization and abstraction.

Winnicott and bisexuality

While many post-Freudian authors use the concept of bisexuality, but without giving it a definitive theoretical status, different consideration must be given to D. W. Winnicott who dedicates to the theme of the bisexuality of human nature some of his greatest and most inspired pages. However, his speculations and trends of thought are complicated and sometimes contradictory, and although they use the classic terminology, they often move away from the Freudian line of thought, without a clarification of all the subtle differences.

In Human Nature (1988; Chapter 1), he in fact speaks of a "part" of the opposite sex—above all, of a "feminine part" of men—that has not been repressed as Freud said (1919), but rather, split off; and this split off part, far from being the lonely imprisonment "of the subordinated sex", would be a potential, dynamic enrichment for the life of the individual.

But then the discourse becomes confused. On the one hand he agrees with the Freudian idea of a common line of development between boy and girl until the phallic phase ("in this stage [pregenital], males and females are not necessarily different"); but then he muddles up the theoretic picture by undoing the link between conflict and drive ("Ambivalence has to deal with the changes of the child's Ego rather than with the development of the id or of the instinct"); thus he redeems corporeal "phases" and "erogenous zones", not through the thrust of the drive vicissitudes, but according to the relative "phantasies" (although, evidently, these phantasies are, in their turn, to be interpreted according to his own personal views, and certainly not to be identified with the classical Kleinian concept of phantasy).

The parameters of "nature" and "culture" then become even more complicated, because while he speaks of human "nature", he also says that the "part" of the opposite sex is in dialectic relation with the capacity to identify with the parents, and that this capacity of identification is in its turn dependent on culture.

> In the case of little girls [. . .] this [full genital capacity] is associated with the capacity for identification with the mother and with women, and in the cultures that turn to this capacity very early on [. . .] the "male in the female" seems to be absent. But the male in the female is always present and important . . . [1988]

I think I can say that, to his way of thinking, human bisexuality rests not so much on biology as on the play of phantasy and on the multiple creative capacities of identification. More of a potentiality to be developed, then, rather than a conflict to be resolved through mutilations and renunciations. Thus, we can probably conclude that maturation and genitality for Freud and for Winnicott go in opposite directions.

But perhaps the divergence lies not so much in the idea of maturation as renunciation or as conquest of the "part" of the opposite sex; but in the fact that Freud speaks of sexuality and bisexuality as drive vicissitudes, while Winnicott moves in a pre-conflictual area of game and illusion in which it is not clear—and this is the problem—whether, when he speaks of "male" and "female" and of "parts of the opposite sex", he is referring to sexuality, to object cathexis, to parental introjections, to stable identifications, or to poetic and metaphysical fictions of a universal intrapsychic dialectic.

In my opinion, the point most susceptible to discussion is when he comes to equate female with pregenital.

... the female side of human nature appeals to the pregenital in a way of which the male side, in the phases of mature genital experience, has no need. [1988, p. 44]

in the case of little girls, there is an inclination to the pregenital much more than in boys. [ibid., p. 46]

Fiction and phantasy in girls is based much more on the pregenital roots and perhaps there is more room for a continuity of the little girl in the category woman than there is for the continuity of boys in the category man. [ibid., p. 49]

On this subject of the archaic levels of sexual gender organization, Winnicott had some of his most poetic intuitions, but he also left room for considerable ambiguity and confusion; for example, by not distinguishing the "female part of the male" from the capacity (which he himself individuated) of the male to identify himself, on one hand, with the "sexed woman", and, on the other hand, with the "woman–mother". In the same way, the relationship between all these aspects of the adult man and his "normal" or "pathological" homosexuality (I am again using his own words) is not clear.

In another of his fundamental works, *Playing and Reality* (1971), it is clear that, in his thinking, there is a strong oscillation between speaking about "male" and "female" as qualities of the actual individual—man or woman—and referring to them as "elements" or symbolic terms of dialectic articulation of opposites in the interpersonal and intrapsychic dimension.

... I associate the impulse referring to the objects (also its passive side) with the masculine element, while I find that what characterizes the feminine element in the context of entering into relations with the object is the identity, that gives the child the basis for being and therefore, later on, the basis for a sense of the self. But I find that, it is here, in the absolute dependence on what the mother provides in the way of that special quality through which she does or does not meet the very first function of the feminine element, that we may search for the foundation of the experience of being. [1971]

It seems that, on this occasion, "feminine" and "masculine" are to be formulated as two metaphoric terms indicating two levels (and not developmental phases!) that then always coexist in dynamic equilibrium. Thus, "feminine" is equal to pregenital and pre-object relations, and "masculine" to object-relatedness.

It is curious how Winnicott, although using profoundly different routes, reaches the same conclusions that Lou Andreas Salome reached in 1914; conclusions that I do not think any psychoanalyst today—whether male or female—would agree with.

Even more Freudian than Freud (like so many of her first generation colleagues), Salome, in her sophisticated, baroque language, sanctions the "naturalness" of women's renunciation of drive fulfilment; in her opinion, the "typical" indulging of women in the "preliminary pleasure" is not perversion, but is a way of embracing with the minimum the totality of the amorous sphere. "The woman remains anchored ... more than the man ... to that primary fusion ..."

By idealizing her, rather than devaluating her, as Freud did, she depicts the woman as a half human being, relegated to an eternal "pregenital" infancy.

We can tolerate these levels of ambiguity and non-discrimination when we have to confront the complexity of reality at a theoretic level; for psychoanalysis itself has taught us that our creative potentials are nourished by doubt and chaos. *But what does it mean if all these confusions overflow into the interpretations that we provide to our patients?*

The levels of feminine/masculine

At the basis of all this tormented and fascinating psychoanalytic speculation about the theme of masculine/feminine and of bisexuality, there is in the human mind an ambivalent tension that cannot be eliminated, and that dates back to the ancient myth of the androgenous and the hermaphrodite.

In fact, it can be seen that we have a profound need to define and to define ourselves according to "gender"; to attribute a masculine or a feminine identity to the world surrounding us, that goes well beyond the specifically sexual field. Many languages, even, extend the distinction of grammatical gender—masculine, feminine, and sometimes neutral—to the whole animate and inanimate world. In some languages (Korean, for example) and in many ancient and modern dialects, the verbal form varies according to whether the individual carrying out the action—in itself completely generic, such as running—is a man or a woman.

However, alongside this need to differentiate and divide, another need is at work—in the opposite direction—the need to remain in confusion and ambiguity. Freud himself included it in a note, subsequently added in 1915, to his famous *Three Essays on the Theory of Sexuality*:

> It is essential to understand clearly that the concepts of "masculine" and "feminine", whose meaning seems so unambiguous to ordinary people, are among the most confused that occur in science. [...] "Masculine" and "feminine" are used ... sometimes in a biological, and sometimes, again, in a sociological sense. [1905, p. 219]

I think it is worth noting that this addition is purposely in reference to one of his most important and subsequently most criticized statements: "... libido is invariably and necessarily of a masculine nature ..."

As we know, Freud claimed that following the vicissitudes of a single libido—masculine—the distinctions and the change towards femininity took place at the oedipal phase. Recent psychoanalytic experience about the early phases of development, however, has privileged the hypothesis of a much earlier, even though primitive and prevalently sensorial possibility of the baby girl or boy to perceive the existence of masculine and feminine in the dimension of the relationship.

Apart from the chronological question, the problem still remains as to whether there is a common line of development that, through symmetrical or asymmetrical vicissitudes, allows for the progressive construction of male and female gender; or whether, right from the beginning, men and women follow different and differentiated developmental processes. In any case, the crucial point is how, and when during the development process, gender identity is grafted onto the process of personal identity, and how the play of impulses, in its turn, interweaves with the definition of gender.

For the sake of clarity, I think it might be useful to try articulating—in a necessarily schematic manner—the problem of human sexuality on various levels (Argentieri, 1988).

1) A first *biological anatomical level* (with the specific genotypical, phenotypical, hormonal, etc. substratum).
2) A second *level of gender*, i.e. *of the psychological feeling of belonging* to the *masculine or the feminine* gender, necessarily articulated in the relationship dimension, both in the relationship with others as similar or different, as well as in the relationship with one's own body.
3) A third *level of the drive vicissitudes*, from which derives the actual acting—or not acting—with specific sexual behaviour.
4) A fourth level regards the *roles and functions* within the socio-cultural environment that are only secondarily sexualized (for example, describing certain emotional or intellectual attitudes or behavioural models as "masculine").
5) Lastly, there is a fifth *metaphoric level*, often used in psycho-analysis, in which some authors speak of "masculine" or "feminine" as analogic, poetic, suggestive extensions of discourse; or as the composite, dialectic duplicity of a single human reality.

It would certainly be utopistic to think that all these levels can coincide in harmonious integration and in step with the development process, and that the passage from corporeal to psychic is made spontaneously, solely by means of a pseudo-evolutionist "internal thrust". Too often, in fact, conflicts and contradictions occur. For instance, the first anatomic–biological level is not sufficient to guarantee the second gender level. We see this in so many clinical situations (or more simply, in so many crises of adolescence) of little, semi-clandestine delusions over a supposed "smallness" of the breast or penis, in which anguished concrete recrimination expresses, at a corporeal level, the feeling of inadequacy and of lack of introjection of the sense of psychological identity.

I believe also that the more the level of psychological gender identity is lacking as authentic personal structure, the greater is the tendency to cling defensively to the biological, corporeal concreteness (such as the categorical necessity of some patients to have an analyst of a certain sex), and consequently to seek reassurance by emphasizing the fourth level—that of socially sexualized roles and functions. Among all these problems and conflicts, the level that risks paying the greatest price is the third one—that of the sexual drives, so often inhibited, impoverished or reduced to sclerotic behaviour.

For, unfortunately, biology is not destiny.

It is not, in itself, sufficient to guarantee the successful develop-ment of the drive vicissitudes, or even the specific construction of sexual gender. Freud himself, and also Anna Freud (on the basis of her experiences with adolescents), both frequently emphasized that the object choice at the origins is by no means determined by sexual gender.

From the psychoanalytic viewpoint, however, the most interesting level is undoubtedly that of gender. For while, according to Freudian theory, drive vicissitudes follow certain internal thrusts, gender is acquired. It is acquired, evidently, not in the old, controversial sense of opposing the congenital to the acquired, but—in a purely psychoanalytic sense—within the relational environment.

Let us think, for example, what personal sense of their own sexual gender mother and father will bring into play in the relationship with their children; which unconscious expectations, projections, delegations, compromises, prohibitions, will be articu-lated in the dual or the triangular relationship within which the child must build his own image?

In this connection, there is a tendency—too hasty in my mind—to individuate a so-called "feminine identification" in homosexual males, based on behavioural rather than psychoanalytical data, as though the same unconscious phantasy always corresponded to a certain way of behaving. *So-called homosexuality*, on the other hand, is only an external aspect to which any number of psychological organizations may correspond. Maintaining that homosexual men are "feminine" is once again equivalent to comparing femininity with indifferentation and regression.

A brief clinical vignette

I think that at this point a brief clinical vignette will help to illustrate my discourse.

A mature patient presents himself for analysis. He is a self-diagnosed homosexual—a condition to which he is very attached. In fact, his sexual life is almost non-existent, and is more or less limited to occasional masturbation, apparently without phantasies.

He is in love with a young man who is not homosexual, and he more or less persecutes him, reproaching him for not returning his affection.

> *He has a dream. His mother (who died several years ago) is cradling an old doll in her arms; she takes no notice of anything that is going on around her. Her son goes towards her and in vain tries to draw her attention. Finally, with great anger and grief, he seizes this doll from her arms, breaks it and destroys it.*

My patient is the last of five children, all males. Thanks to this dream, we were able to understand how he had always felt that his mother wanted him to be a girl, and in her heart she had never accepted him.

I think that when he tore the old doll from his mother's arms he was expressing his desperate protest against her narcissistic refusal to renounce her wish for a little girl, with whom she could live a total fusional experience. As just another male child, he had been neither loved nor accepted.

In his love for the young man, therefore, I by no means see a so-called "homosexual choice", in which my patient puts into play his feminine identification. On the contrary, I think that he desperately wants to repeat and actualize his drama. He cannot be loved on account of his masculine sex; today, the boy, in the same way as his mother in the past, would only be able to love a girl. Thus, he defends and tries to preserve his gender—his male being—through angry and indomitable protest; but at the price of annulling his sexual drives. And so his gender is saved, as one might say, but at the expense of his impulses.

As I said at the beginning, it is unfortunately anything but rare for sexuality and gender identity, instead of promoting and reinforcing, to reciprocally obstruct each other.

Identification and disidentification

Let us return, therefore, to a problem that is continually coming up in our discussion on bisexuality: that of the identifications/disidentifications that boys and girls are able to make regarding their parents, and particularly the so-called "primary identification" of both the boy and the girl with the mother. The concept of identity and other co-related concepts (introjection, incorporation, imitation, adhesive

THE AMBIGUITY OF BISEXUALITY IN PSYCHOANALYSIS

and projective identification, etc.) are certainly some of the most complex and controversial in psychoanalysis; and, according to the various reference models of psychoanalytic theory, are currently the subject of numerous critical revisions that we cannot go into here.

On this point of primary identification, the complexity of the problems and the theoretical divergences seem to have been forgotten in order to maintain a state of generic agreement, at least at the level of clinical interpretations: that is, that women would appear to be helped in the construction of their feminine identity by their so-called primary identification with the mother, taking for granted that this primary phase of non-distinction between self and mother is at least in linear sequence with—even though not analogous to—an adult identity. I refer particularly to the well-known work by Greenson (1968). Briefly, the author begins with Freud's thesis, according to which the little girl has to elaborate two important conflictual areas from which the little boy is exempt: changing the erogenous zone from clitoris to vagina, and changing love object from mother to father. But, Greenson observes:

> the male child, in order to attain a healthy sense of maleness, must replace the primary object of his identification, the mother, and must identify instead with the father. I believe it is the difficulties inherent in this additional step of development, from which girls are exempt, which are responsible for certain special problems in the man's gender identity [...]. The girl too must dis-identify from mother if she is to develop her own unique identity, but her identification with mother *helps* her establish her femininity. [1968, p. 370]

For my part, I have several doubts about the supposed advantage that this so-called primary identification with the mother is said to represent in the feminine development process (Argentieri, 1985). Freud (1921) very rarely used the term of primary identification, referring instead to "the earliest expression of an emotional tie with another person", a form of bond "in the early history of the Oedipus complex" that is direct and immediate and does not expect object investment; while secondary identifications that come about later and are structuring were, in his opinion, the result of the Oedipus complex. Certainly, at the time of these Freudian conceptualizations, the very early development vicissitudes had not yet been described; but it is evident that Freud did not fail to emphasize the archaic, pre-object-related and non-sexual nature of this mechanism: "... in these identifications, the Ego sometimes copies the person" (Freud, 1921); and further on he specifies that a distinction must be made between what the boy wants to be (identification with the father) and what he wants to have (the mother as a sexually cathected object).

In his work on "On transference" (1956), Winnicott is in agreement with this interpretation of Freudian thought. While investigating "towards a deeper insight into this matter of the mother with her infant", he says that "... 'primary identification' implies an environment that is not yet differentiated from that which will be the individual" (p. 386). I, therefore, think that we should by no means take for granted that women have an advantage over men regarding the development of the acquisition of adult gender identity, because of their so-called primary identification with the mother. Such an "identification" is only an undifferentiated, fusional situation, allowing perhaps for only an imitative pseudo-femininity that—at a conscious level—could be reassurance of having reached an adult age; whereas to achieve a genuine gender identity, it is necessary first to have accomplished the initial stage of separation from the mother, and then a differentiation between father and mother, male and female. But, whereas the developmental thrust and the perception of his own concrete male corporeity can assist a boy towards differentiation from the mother, for a girl, growing up and becoming a woman—and therefore the same as the mother—can acquire the significance of "being" the mother and of feeling recaptured by the primitive fusional bond (Pines, 1992).

By preserving these terms of primary identification and the corresponding disidentification, ambiguity and confusion are enhanced, as if, for a little girl, the so-called primary identification with the mother could be considered equivalent to a kind of primitive acquisition of female gender. Failure to successfully complete this separation and differentiation process is just as catastrophic for the development of a woman as it is for that of a man. Otherwise, *another link is added to the chain of misunderstandings: the woman as* *"castrated male", as eternal pregenital child, as undifferentiated creature* with the ambiguous consolation of bisexuality.

As we have already said, however, the great problem is to

understand how and when, during the course of development, gender identity—whether male or female—is grafted onto and articulated in the process of personal identity. It is true that everything starts from the corporeal, from the earliest sensorial experiences; and that from the very first stages of life, when the boundary between self and the other has not yet been defined, both boy and girl babies are already able to mentally register intuitions and sensations about the difference between males and females. But this does not mean the ability either to individuate the mother as female or to categorize, from birth, "male" and "female" in an "adult" anatomical and psychological sense. A more likely hypothesis is that, only at a later stage, during the individuation and differentiation processes, does a re-categorization of the primitive experiences and phantasies in terms of male and female occur at more integrated levels, as "retroactive, effect" (*Nachträglichkeit*).[4]

At the origins, therefore, at the stage of the so-called primary identifications (but also, as we have learned from our clinical experience, at adult stages of life if pathological developments have not allowed for adequate maturation), the maternal image, far from being "female", can only be confused and composed of attributes and functions that are together "maternal" and "paternal".

Disentangling from the primary maternal image that which is paternal, and attributing it to the true father, is a complex and difficult task. We often see how our patients, during the course of this process, have remained entrapped in errors, in compromises and in intermediary defensive organizations that have only the appearance of a heterosexual adult relationship.

The primal scene

The primal scene, therefore, retains all its importance as a universal drama and as an essential crossroads for maturation, although it is articulated for each individual in a personal, unique, and unrepeatable interweaving of real perceptions and phantasies. It is not an "event", but a "process" that constantly accompanies the vicissitudes of object relations and instinctuality, from the initial indifferentiation between self and mother, or between self and objective world, towards a gradual possibility—marked by continual oscillations and regressions—of perceiving the "other"—the father—not only as an image that is initially equivalent to and superimposed on the maternal image, but as a "second object" that is distinct as well as separate from the mother and from the self.

As we know, real perceptions and the related phantasies of sexual intercourse between adults do not automatically acquire for the child the quality of a "triangular" relationship; and also the so-called derivates of the primal scene—screen memories, dreams, symptoms—will reflect the level at which the infantile mind has tried to assign meaning to the perturbing event or events.

Thus, before the three-sided relationship is firmly structured in the infant psyche, and before the full explosion of the oedipal drama, recognition of the father, of the "masculine" (male) as second object, can only be experienced, as our everyday clinical experience teaches us, as an unexpected and disconcerting series of changes in the first object—the mother. This is the age of nightmares, of the unknown and overwhelming imaginary figures in which the so-called "combined parental" and composite image can appear as a single creature twice its size and with two sets of limbs; or the early attempts to distinguish and divide can be expressed by phantasies of more or less bloody mutilations and cutting in half of the first image. However, the mother, unrecognizable and therefore monstrous, always appears as threatening inasmuch as she marks the abrupt preclusion to a hitherto privileged relationship of fusional union.

We must not forget that the elaboration of the primal scene is the essential presupposition to differentiation between male and female, and therefore to the acquisition of a personal and structured gender identity; a process that requires the capacity to recognize not only that which is similar to the self, but also that which is different. Before a final distinction between father and mother, male and female, can be accomplished in the infantile mind, pseudo-differentations and unequal splits into two images can take place. Beginning with the "monstrous" mother (the combined-parental figure), these can attribute certain qualities and functions to one sex or the other; for example, instinctual aspects can be split and projected onto the father and onto males in general, while the female maternal image may be preserved from conflict and ambivalence.

For instance, this is often the neurotic "solution" at the base of many organizations of female homosexuality, when an attempt is made to avoid the levels of conflict and instinctuality by excluding males from love relationships. Perhaps we can give the same interpretation to the symptom of Freud's patient in "Hysterical phantasies and their relationship to bisexuality", to which we have already referred (1908, p. 6). Rather than a concrete representation of bisexuality, the symptom could be understood as a use of the body as a theatre for the primal scene; an enacting of the relationship male/female, father/mother, burdened by conflict and aggressiveness all concentrated on one of the components of the couple.

An author who has given much thought to very early mental processes and to the importance of the primal scene in the psychosexual development process, is Eugenio Gaddini. In many of his works he describes the acquisition of identity as a process; not in the everyday chronological and deterministic sense, but as the result of progressive moments of introjection relative to the possibility of living conflictual and instinctual levels (psycho-oral area) in the dimension of the dual and then the triangular relationship. Moreover, parallel to the introjective processes, Gaddini individuates the imitative processes (psychosensorial area) that, on the contrary, operate in the service of fusionality and omnipotence in an a-conflictual, magical dimension that rapidly achieves the illusion of "being" the object, without going through the anguish of separation and growth.

As Gaddini himself always emphasized, imitation is a precious physiological component in the process of identity construction, if it is integrated with and subordinate to the introjective processes. To this healthy quota of the imitative processes we may attribute our capacity for empathy and resonance; our episodic possibility of "being" the other—also the other sex—in order to understand him or her. If, on the other hand, imitations prevail and are stably organized, specific pathologies result in which, behind the imitative facade (sometimes very efficient on the exterior), are hidden the fragility and the precarious nature of the structure.

Thus, in the case of sexual gender also, it is only by means of a long and harmonious process of introjection that identity gender can be reached. On the other hand, many "imitations" of masculinity and femininity that, through their rigid and stereotyped quality evidence the lack of genuine roots of identity, can be traced back to the fact that psycho-sensorial, magical mechanisms have prevailed.

There is a type of "clandestine" pathology, for instance, specific to certain women—especially of the past generation—whose drives were dramatically mutilated and sacrificed in favour of a facade of "normality". A "normality" in whose name, so it appears, they went through all the stages of adult femininity (sexual intercourse, childbirth, etc.) in a manner that was highly satisfying at conscious levels—both to the women and to their partners, in one of those states of "perfect disequilibrium" of a couple that can achieve the most tenacious resistential aspects.

A "wild card" at the service of defence mechanisms

To conclude these reflections, I think I can say that the concept of bisexuality, with all its theoretical ambiguity and fragility, has maintained its fortune intact throughout the years, because it is able to clandestinely serve the defences of both the patient and the analyst.

As each of us will have learned from personal clinical experience, sometimes the "temperature" in the transference/counter-transference) can become "hot" in the sexuality field. When this happens, an "explanation" in terms of general bisexuality can offer, to either member of the analytic couple, a temporary relief from the anxieties of the relationship.

For example, this is what happened to a young patient of mine who, in a delicate phase of the analysis, when he was beginning to have strong ambivalent desires of passivity towards me, began to feel attracted by transvestite streetwalkers. "I think we have touched my bisexual levels", he suggested compunctiously, trying by means of a kind of intellectual collusion to dilute the tension that had been created between us through a universal bisexual destiny.

Another example derives from the clinical case of a colleague that I discussed during a scientific meeting. The clinical material regarded the last session before the summer holidays of a woman patient who, for a long time, had wanted to have a baby; but instead of this, she was going to have a meiomectomy that very summer.

The patient was very upset, and she told of a dream in which she was with a woman who tried to seduce her in an atmosphere of great sexual excitement; but the patient had refused her. The analyst (a man) had had no difficulty in understanding that he himself was the woman in the dream, and he had also told this to his patient. But then, instead of interpreting the problem in the transference and within the framework of the dramatic separation coinciding with the surgical operation, he had considered it more opportune to offer an interpretation regarding the woman's unconscious conflicts about her sexual object choices directed towards males or females. He had added that this led back to her basic unconscious bisexuality, of which she was now less afraid, to the extent that she could let it emerge in a dream. In our discussion, the analyst justified his interpretative choice by the need to contain the patient's anxiety about the imminent separation. Faced with the emergence of aggressive eroticized aspects in the transference, at the moment when the painful problem of the drive relationship with the primitive, undifferentiated mother is reactivated, and the patient is exposed to confused and uncontrolled tensions, the analyst—so I believe—preferred to be on the side of the patient's defences by suggesting an interpretation of bisexuality.

Displacing the problem *outside the relationship* can push back into the unconscious and thus appease both the original conflict as well as that reactualized in the transference (in fact, in this case, the analyst said that the woman became calmer); but this defensive operation of annulling the tension always has its price. In fact, it leads back to the problem at that universal "biological" level that Freud (1937) purposely defined as "not analyzable", and therefore outside processuality and development.

Indeed, by invoking the concept of bisexuality, it is possible for the patient—but also for the analyst—to avail himself of the "convenient possibility of constantly switching his associations, as though on to an adjoining track, into the field of the contrary meaning" (Freud, 1908). Thus, in my opinion, he is able to express not an indomitable biological bisexuality, but a defensive, specifically psychological splitting between parts of the self and the analytic relationship.

The sexual gender of the analyst

In conclusion, when we are faced with the problem of the analyst's capacity to enter into a deep relationship with his patients of either sex and at the various levels of their primary relationships with both parents, I wonder—always in the name of the ambiguous concept of bisexuality—whether we are not demanding a paradox of ourselves. On the one hand, we expect every analyst to have achieved his own specific gender identity—differentiated and mature; on the other hand, we invoke his (or her) readiness to be both father and mother, male and female, for his or her patients.

But the hypothesis, analogous with the double embryonic potentiality, that every human being is able to let emerge in himself a supposed psychological "part" corresponding to the opposite sex, seems to me to be more of an inheritance from a mythological nostalgia for the lost hermaphrodite perfection rather than a real psychological possibility.

I am inclined to believe that every analyst should be ready to regress temporarily with his patient to those indifferentiated all-powerful levels at which the endopsychic separation between mother and father, between masculine and feminine, has not yet taken place; but only as a premise to the difficult road ahead should we accept the limit of our own gender identity, and of that which can only be known through the relationship with the other, with someone different from the self. Otherwise, if the anxiety about integration and conflict is too strong, we may give in to the temptation of defensive regression towards those primitive, undifferentiated states where the pangs of being divided are not suffered, where the illusion of being "everything" hides the painful truth of being "nothing; a nostalgia for the perfection of a lost paradise where—like the angels and with the alibi of bisexuality—the dilemma of which sex one belongs to can remain unsolved for ever.

Notes

1. This paper "El sexo de los ángeles: la ambigüedad de la bisexualidad en el psicoanálisis" has been published in Spanish in *Mujeres por Mujeres*, Biblioteca peruana de Psicoanálisis, Lima, Moisés Lemlij, editor. 1994, pp. 146–168.
2. As will be remembered, it was Freud's young patient, Emma Eckstein, alias Irma, who suffered most from this eccentric theory. Following a diagnosis of "wish epistaxis", Fliess operated on her nasal cavities, and she nearly died on account of an infection and haemorrhage caused by a

piece of gauze that had been left in the wound.

This dramatic episode is recorded in great detail in certain letters that Anna Freud and Marie Bonaparte held back from publication to "protect the master's image". The foolish secret was then ably exploited by Masson, who had gained access to the Freud Archives, in order to produce his well-known scandalistic speculation.

The positive side of the matter, however, is that we now have the possibility of establishing certain new meaningful connections. For example, the defensive importance for Freud himself of being able to sponsor the hypothesis of a "natural" bisexuality of all human beings, in respect of his own homosexual anxieties towards his idealized interlocutor to whom—his feelings of guilt about poor Emma summarily placated—he was able to write during those same years: "Nessuno può sostituire per me la compagnia dell'amico, che una mia parte—forse femminile—reclama ..." [Letter of Freud to Fliess: 7 May 1990, p. 452].

3. I think it is interesting to recall that this fundamental work of Freud (1919) is largely based on the analysis of his daughter, Anna, and that Anna herself in "The relation of beating phantasies to a day-dream" (1922) included her own scarcely disguised personal "clinical case" among those of the six anonymous children that it deals with. She thus provides definite confirmation of Sigmund's theories, that infantile phantasies of being beaten are an expression of past desires of love for the father, transformed by guilt feelings and neurotic processes into conscious phantasies of a masochistic nature.

Although Anna herself provided most of the material, both father and daughter speak essentially about the developmental process of little boys.

In the same way, if we compare "Some psychical consequences of the anatomical difference between the sexes" (1925) by Sigmund, with the brief presentation on "Jealousy and desire of masculinity" that Anna made almost at the same time, we see that both of them investigate the psychosexual development of the little girl along the same lines as that of the boy.

Contrary, to all the other first generation women psychoanalysts, Anna did not write anything specifically on the sexuality of women; an omission, to my mind, that signifies even more her complete adherence to Sigmund's first hypotheses on the subject of femininity.

In a recent work (Anna Freud, la figlia", in Psicoanalisi al Femminile, 1992) I have tried to describe the defensive collusion between Freud and his daughter in the area of the undifferentiated primary relationship rather than at the oedipal level. This is perhaps another example of how the capacity to theorize can be conditioned by our most intimate vicissitudes.

4. In virtue of all these considerations, I think it is more convincing to formulate the process of psychosexual development in the light of the concept of "retroactive effect" (*Nachträglichkeit*), rather than that of "very early oedipal" (Szpilka, 1985; Argentieri, 1985; Amati, *et al.*, 1990) that is, as an experience that on one hand acquires meaning according to previous events and phantasies, while, on the other hand, in its turn retroactively resignifies the past.

CHAPTER SEVEN

The woman clinician in clinical work with infants and adults

Frances Thomson-Salo

I n this chapter I am starting on an exploration of whether there is a difference between women and men clinicians in their experiencing and response to affects, an exploration of the use of ourselves in interaction with our patients. As the starting point, I have taken infant–parent psychotherapy as practised in Europe, the United States, and Australia.

Clinicians increasingly recognize that when parents and infants experience difficulties in the early years it is important to treat not only the parents' difficulties and depression. The infant and the mother–infant relationship also need therapeutic input to ensure optimal outcomes. Yet the infant's distress is often only communicated somatically. Working psychoanalytically with the infant present, affects technique in that the clinician may need to respond physically to the infant, and to work with their own feelings about this as well as any discomfort about not working in more traditional ways. With a distressed mother *and* a distressed infant in the room, we need to be aware of how differently the body may do the feeling and thinking in this interaction than in adult work. Joan Raphael-Leff (2001) highlighted the need to remember the unity of the mind and the body of both the clinician and those seeking help. This work, therefore, relies considerably on the clinician's receptiveness to the total emotional and physical responses taking place in mother, infant, and clinician.

Having a body, whether of the same or of a different sex, with its own physical experiences will have an effect on the clinical work. Women are biologically primed to resonate with the infant's communication from pregnancy onwards. It can be argued on evolutionary grounds that women are genetically programmed to build stronger relationships in virtually all cultures for the sake of survival of the species, because if they did not attach, babies would not survive. I am suggesting that women clinicians, whether or not they have had children, will be similarly primed to resonate with the infant's communication (and the infant-in-the-adult). This is not to suggest that the capacity to resonate empathically is the prerogative of women, or indeed that it is always freely available to them. I also want to acknowledge how much sensitive work is done by gifted male clinicians and how much overlap there is, in the way men and women respond. But I will look primarily at what a woman clinician brings to the work, and whether there are gender differences in the response to affects experienced. I will refer briefly to some empirical research and finish by touching on the relevance to clinical work with adults.

I will look first at what is needed in working with infants and their parents who are experiencing difficulties. Here, the fantasy of whom the baby represents often overrides the mother's ability to intuitively understand her child.

Infant–parent psychotherapy

In infant–parent psychotherapy the clinician works, in the infant's presence, with the parents' anxiety or distorting projections. She is seen as present in her own right, and related to in an attempt to alter her representations. Outwardly this may seem to consist of little more than facial or hand gestures on the clinician's part, following the infant's play and talking to her. The therapeutic factor, as in adult work, is the clinician's thinking about the infant and communicating this. As the therapist's response conveys that there is an undamaged part of the infant, the mother feels mothered and a good internal object reappears.

It may help to give an example here (Thomson-Salo *et al.*, 1999).

> About twenty years ago Ann Morgan, a paediatrician at the Royal Children's Hospital, Melbourne, was consulted about a seven-week-old gaze-avoidant girl, Alana. Her parents thought she was blind, deaf and autistic. The mother had previously worked with autistic infants. The father thought there was some response to him although he was losing hope because of the baby's withdrawal. In a home movie of bath time, Alana, who had always been unable to look at her mother, had rolled over so that she was looking at the camera. The water was lapping over her face but she was not struggling. Her parents were totally unaware of this.

When Ann Morgan first saw the infant, she said

> "she was wrapped in her blanket and cocooned, her hands lying very passively on the blanket, her eyes closed and sucking on the dummy, very unresponsive with all of us standing around the cot. The first thing I did was to talk to her very quietly, barely above a whisper and she stopped sucking immediately. Then I held onto her hand and stroked it a bit while I was talking to her. Unbelievably, she began to stroke my finger and then her own finger and it was as if she could feel both fingers, and she kept stroking her own finger and stroking my finger. All the time I was talking to her I was certain she heard me, that she was in fact aware of the other, but also was making the other aware of her. I think it meant a great deal to the mother when we talked about the fact that her daughter could hear perfectly well, that she was very aware of me and was, I think, both thinking about it and being very separate and thoughtful."

It would have been difficult to work only with the parents' representations when their difficulties were already having such an effect on their interaction with their daughter. What Ann Morgan did in connecting with the infant was to unhook the projections sufficiently, so that mother and daughter could reconnect.

Infant–parent psychotherapy is usually short-term because of the fluidity in the parent–infant system and the infant is often extraordinarily responsive. The clinician needs to be comfortable working with regression in the mother as well as the infant's non-verbal communication. With "no language but a cry", the psychosomatic "language" is the infant's first language. The clinician relies on being able to quickly read her total emotional and physical responses.

The core principle of infant–parent psychotherapy is to "be with the infant", relating to her as a subject in her own right, not as an object of investigation, and discovering her irreducible uniqueness. As Ann Morgan said:

> In the intersubjectivity between the child and myself, I know that the infant understands that I understand, and she knows that what she is getting is communication ... It's important for me to know what the baby sees in me as well as what I see in the baby and it's that link between us that really holds us together and that can quite often hold the baby. I can feel the link with the baby, that the baby has cottoned on to me and I have cottoned on to the baby, and then I can begin to talk to the baby.

> With a baby who's continually on the breast, the link between mother and baby has broken down so that the baby has to be on the breast ... and there's no gap (a transitional space). Then the baby's eye contact with you means that there is a gap. What I think is important about helping the mother see this link, is that it allows a space in which something can appear: in the mother's mind a thought, in the baby a beginning of a preconception; the baby has a feeling that she is there in her own right. The baby has a contact that is separate from and not through her mother, which in turn helps the mother realize that there is some separation between them. There is a look of relief on the baby's face and on the mother's, which can be seen as early as four months. [Thomson-Salo & Paul, 2001, pp. 46–47]

The clinician works actively at making a connection with the infant: if, for example, you hold out a toy so that even a young baby can hold it, and then gently pull back, the baby has an awareness of someone who recognizes her agency. She can then sense it for herself, which is extremely significant. The clinician's physical and emotional response is particularly relevant where she makes an emotional contact with the infant to bring about change, with non-verbal ways of relating. Attuning to the infant's affect when the infant is despairing or angry conveys "I know what you feel because I feel it too", that she is being responded to as a subject, which brings hope and often a quick response. Playfulness has probably the greatest potential to give the infant hope.

What is evoked in clinicians when intuitively they choose a particular way of relating and playing?

Gender in clinical work

I think we have, to some extent, ignored the relevance of gender, firstly, of the infant, and as Brigid Jordan (1997) says, treated female and male infants as though they brought identical issues to a therapeutic encounter. And yet researchers have found differences between female and male babies from birth. Whereas girls are generally more self-contained, boys tend to be more dependent on their mothers for help in managing their feelings of joy and anger. When they have depressed mothers they feel more angry and deprived. How girl and boy infants relate differently is likely to affect the clinician's response to them.

Secondly, have we to some extent left on one side the question of how the clinician's gender affects their response? While Chasseguet-Smirgel (1986) wrote that the analyst's counter-transference is assumed to be different between the two sexes, she added that for the male analyst, the femininity of the analyst is needed for the capacity to wait and watch a relationship develop, which blurs the differences. Perhaps anxiety about losing the gains of the theory of psychic bisexuality has hindered further exploration, or our theories have blinkered us.

For example, it is usually maintained that the clinician's gender does not significantly affect the emerging transferences. Ruth Safier (personal communication) suggested a further reason. Women struggle to recognize that their vulnerability and openness to counter-transference experience represents a strength, similar to how mothers of infants are usually unaware of what a difficult task they are doing until it is validated.

We listen with our bodies with a gendered mind. Koutas and Federmeier (1998) wrote:

> The brain is but one component of the complex system that is the body. We take in information and interact with the world though our own bodies, and our bodies change with—and in some cases change—cognitive and emotional processing. [p. 135]

Stern (2000) put it succinctly: "all mental acts (perception, feeling, cognition, remembering) are accompanied by input from the body" (p. xviii). How could we, for so long, have left the body out of our thinking about the clinician?

The woman clinician in infant–parent psychotherapy

I am suggesting that as mothers are primed physically and emotionally to respond to infants, this is a biological sensitivity which women have. A woman clinician engaged in infant–parent psychotherapy is able to respond to infants out of this sensitivity. She is also able to identify with and respond to the mothers, including the infant-in-the mother, i.e. to be in touch in a deep way with regression.

Attunement

Before outlining some data to consider whether women and men listen differently, I'll give an example from the work of another infant mental health clinician at the Royal Children's Hospital.

> Michele Meehan, Maternal and Child Health Nurse, was consulted about an eleven-month-old boy who was furious that his mother wanted to wean him. His mother had been trying to introduce other food from six months of age but he had refused everything except breast milk. The constant breast-feeding was tiring her. Once she started to wean him from the breast, he refused the bottle and all food, refused to be held by his mother when she did not let him feed, hit her, and pulled her hair. He screamed and threw things at her when he woke in the morning; he did not accept any of her

overtures. His mother was distraught and tearful. Michele had talked this through with her but it had no effect. Then when he wanted to feed and his mother refused, he reached out and hit her. Michele commented to his mother, "He's really angry with you." He then picked up a softball, and flung it, yelling, at his mother, and then clenched his lips. Michele caught the ball and, attuning to his anger and matching it, she flung the ball back to the foot of the cot.

He was instantly engaged, recognized the communication, smiled, and returned the ball to Michele for them both to play a throwing game. It developed gradually into a quieter tossing and catching game which he let his mother join in. With his next feed it was noticeable that his anger had gone, he was able to accept food from his mother and the good relationship was evident.

The meaning to the infant of the loss of the breast had contributed to the mother's difficulties in thinking. When the mother could not break the deadlock Michele was able to reconnect them. She intuitively knew that, in play, the infant's rage at the mother could be accepted and survived. She had attuned to the infant's anger in such a way that he could hear the communication (Thomson-Salo *et al.*, 1999).

To think further about attunement, let us turn to studies of mother–infant interaction. Researchers view the exquisite turn-taking between mother and infant more within a model of a single mind than Bion's model of two minds trying to get together. The single-mind model bears out the idea of women being primed for emotional communication. If mothers are equipped to attune to infants, women clinicians would have this to draw on.

Research on mirror neurons in the premotor cortex (which provide a basis for feeling in the body an action which someone else did) and adaptive oscillators (which synchronize our movements to those of others) seem confirmatory of a primary intersubjectivity in which the newborn is primed for face-to-face communication. Across cultures, mothers talk to their infants, and not just their own, in "motherese", in which their voice rises as much as two octaves. Fathers' voices also rise but not as much. Blum (1997) argues that:

infants turn more readily towards a woman's high-note sounds
than towards the tones the same woman might use to an adult. And
the heart of the infant slows, calms, and steadies ... the comfort that
mother gives child appears basic, biological, and continuous with
(perhaps part of) the same developmental process which goes on in
the womb. It is in this intertwining of mother and child ... that the
evolutionary argument for emotional differences between men and
women begins. [p. 69]

The work of Davidson and Fox (1982) with older infants
suggests that the mere perception of emotion in the partner creates
a resonant emotional state in the self. They studied ten-month-old
infants as they watched videos of a laughing or crying actor, with
simultaneous EEG activation of the corresponding left or right
frontal lobe.

Subsequent research suggests a neurological basis for mother–
infant non-verbal emotional sharing. Siegel (2001) wrote:

As the right hemisphere both sends and receives these signals, the
opportunity is created for a "resonance" of the minds of each of the
individuals. At this non-verbal, core-self level, the interaction of self
with other becomes mapped in the brain in a manner that literally,
neurologically, creates the mind of the other. [p. 84]

This emotionally attuned communication allows the infant to "feel
felt", creating a secure attachment. Schore (2000, personal communication) considered whether mothers might carry out a containing
function differently from fathers. He thought there would be both
quantitative and qualitative differences in the effects of adult female
and male brains on the infant's brain, with an initial heavier
influence from the mother in the early years.

Carrying the baby *in utero* starts the process of being receptive
to raw emotional states and transforming them. Fathers, too, will
draw on their own experience of having been a baby, to perform
this function. What is different about mothers' capacity for
attunement, identification, and containment is that having carried
the infant in their body, their communications to one another
have been known for a long time. Women also elaborate their
fantasies preconsciously for years, carrying the infant, "*my
baby*", in their mind since their own infancy. A mother can then

function with delicate tendrils coming from the newborn. This would be a psychobiological preparedness for attuned containing communication.

Gender differences in empathy have also been explored. Baron-Cohen (cited in Carter, 2000) wrote that: "ascribing mental states to other people (is) an area in which normal females outstrip normal males" (p. 123). Hoffman (1978) found that day-old female infants cried more intensely at the sound of other babies crying than did boy infants, and he likened this empathic response to an underground stream running through women's lives. Similarly, Lieberman (2000) noted:

> There is strong and consistent evidence that women are better encoders and decoders of non-verbal communication ... and this evidence has frequently been cited as possible evidence for women's intuition. [p. 126]

What might underlie this neurologically? Carter (2000) wrote that:

> The corpus callosum—the band of tissue through which the two hemispheres communicate—is relatively larger in women than in men. So is the anterior commissure—a more primitive connection between the hemispheres that links the unconscious areas of the hemispheres only. This may explain why women seem to be more aware of their own and others' emotions than men—the emotionally sensitive right hemisphere is able to pass more information to the analytical linguistically talented left side. It may also allow emotion to be incorporated more easily into speech and thought processes. [p. 108]

(It is also suggested that some structural differences between women's and men's eyes is linked with the particular kind of contemplative gaze with which mothers hold their infants.)

When a clinician touches an infant there is a dialogue of feelings in the infant's "language", which the clinician joins in receptively and containingly. When Jessica James (personal communication) describes reaching out with her hand to touch a baby, feeling protective towards his mother whose son was manifesting her internal squirming and resisting, James communicates something very different from trying merely to settle an infant. Where the clinician is receptive to the infant's fear, and communicates safety (and pleasure) to her, this can be immensely therapeutic.

Regression

Having outlined a case for women's capacity for attunement, it follows that there is a greater ease to identify with regressive and infantile states in clinical work.

With both the mother and the infant painfully in distress in the consulting room, how much more likely is it that the clinician's response will be more on the borders of psyche and soma? I have been struck by how often clinicians working with mothers and infants describe physical responses, e.g. feeling panicky in identification with the infant, or experiencing a pain in the chest from the mother's unacknowledged sadness. Such experiences will impact on our responses. I hear about these physical feelings more from women clinicians. They have been surprised at finding themselves overwhelmed with hunger after seeing a depressed mother or a young child who tried so hard to be so pretty, so good, and so engaging. One clinician said, "it's a gut feeling, the baby's distress becomes mine, it's very powerful, I began to feel what it was like to be the baby, and then to feel sick". This seems comparable to mothers being in tune with the infant's lost, frightened and vulnerable feelings. The adult's capacity for attuned regression means the infant is more readily understood, and the infant's state tolerated, by the mother and the clinician.

We can turn to the experience of a woman preparing to have a baby to see if there are parallels. The regression of primary maternal preoccupation is likely to be underpinned by hormonal changes. With birth, the release of oxytocin, in particular, allows patterns of nursing and caring to appear. Oxytocin may cause anxiety at the loss of identity and self control as it undoes the neural connections so that new experience can form (Carter, 2000). We need to take seriously the woman's confusion and her somatic experience, that she has to wait until what she is experiencing makes sense, until there is an integration of some knowing about the baby and herself as mother. This can be seen as her total vulnerability, that, as a mother, she relinquishes control of her mind in order to accommodate the infant, trusting she will recover it again. Paradoxically it is also her strength—to allow this vulnerability. Again there seems to be a gender difference as men seem less to identify with the confusion. Clinical experience suggests that in infant–parent work women's responses carry a hallmark that is more direct and felt in the body, whereas that of men may seem more distanced in the thinking conveyed, while this may offer a needed space. (Further endocrine studies may elucidate whether a hormonally-driven female bonding response, different from that available in men, has implications for women clinicians working with women.)

If clinicians can stay with not-understanding the infant, this conveys to mother and infant that they can survive and it is safe to wait. In tuning into the infant's psychosomatic language, a woman brings her experience of having to accommodate to her own body feelings, such as feeling out of control with menstruation, before regaining an equilibrium. The pull to merge, because of the sameness of the woman therapist with the mother, to sink back into the mother and be cared for, helps the woman clinician to empathize and identify. The regression in the mother may, however, exert a regressive pull in the clinician, which she needs to remain in control of. When a woman clinician resonates physically and emotionally with a mother and infant, she needs to monitor what is happening while trusting her often intuitive response.

Other clinical work

It seems likely that women clinicians take this biological sensitivity into clinical work with adult patients. Women's comfort with the modality of touch may give rise to preconscious images in the counter-transference that can guide interpretation. Women clinicians, working with adults, report that they describe themselves feeling more lost and confused about what is happening in sessions than men clinicians. While cultural factors may contribute to this openness, women's ease with not-knowing seems comparable to mothers being in tune with the infant's vulnerable, frightened, and lost feelings and able to bear them. Safier (personal communication) suggests a lessened omnipotence for women analysts and women in general, because of physical experiences of loss of control and fragility.

Tronick *et al.*'s (1998) thinking about the factors that bring about therapeutic change, in addition to interpretations, is relevant. He thought that the interpretation would be carried in a moment of authentic person-to-person meeting where the person had an experience of really being "met and known". He thought this would be similar to moments in mother–infant interaction where the infant had a subjective feeling of fulfilment at being "met and known". The woman clinician has had the experience of having once been an infant, and a physical and emotional endowment as a woman to be in touch with infantile communication, either directly from an infant or the infant-in-the adult.

Drawing on mother–infant studies and clinical experience, I have looked at how this suggests that women respond differently. I have not explored the evolving dance between the gender of the clinician and the person who consults them. It would seem likely that as we are seen and known—in our bodies and personalities—much more than we realize, this privileges which kind of transference–counter-transference develops. It seems likely that there are significant differences in style of relating when the psychoanalytic dyad is male–male, female–female or female–male. Common perceptions suggest that females seek much more overt emotional exchange and female–male relationships are more charged with sexual tension. Confiding emotions have tended to go against the grain of male relationships, and feelings of competition and rivalry need to be overcome. In these relationships, interpersonal difficulties are accompanied by high states of anxiety. Women, with the experience of a good analysis with a male analyst, sometimes express the wish to have a second analysis with a woman in order to "go deeper". Whether the ensuing emotional differences are significant remains to be further explicated.

Researchers have explored how the experience of relating affects both partners neurologically. The clinical encounter is not identical with the mother–infant one, but modes of relating and communicating are likely to persist throughout life and to be especially important in significant encounters, such as the clinical. We need to be mindful of what we bring as a gendered clinician. Perhaps the research findings will help us explore how gender might affect the different physicality with which women and men listen and respond to feelings aroused in them in infant–parent psychotherapy and other clinical work.

CHAPTER EIGHT

The "green continent": the constitution of femininity in a clinical case[1]

Teresa Rocha Leite Haudenschild

> "One could compare a woman in her various manifestations
> with a tree whose fruits cannot be gathered, separated,
> packaged, and sent off as if they were products for different
> purposes. The fruits have to be seen as the tree's global
> expression in its process of blossoming and maturing; in the
> global beauty of the shade it provides, through the simple
> fact of its being there, of acting. It is something from which
> new blossoms and new trees are constantly sprouting ... In
> fact, it's the absence of pride that produces its natural
> greatness, which is the clear awareness that there is no need
> to make this kind of assertions [competing with men] in order
> to feel the sublime justification of being a woman and realize
> that one only needs to reach out as far as one's shade ..."
>
> Lou Andreas Salome, 1899

I nstead of being defined by comparison with a man ("without a
penis", or "castrated"—Freud, 1924b), a woman here is
compared to a tree—in all its plenitude and singularity. This
definition is based not on things men *do*, but simply on *being*, like a
tree that produces other trees, fruit, and shade. Instead of being seen

as a "dark continent" (Freud, 1924—December 29), an obscure area, femininity is compared to a vigorous green continent, like a great virgin forest with its countless trees. This metaphor will be used as a background in this text which, like any other text, will cast light on new territories to the extent that it uncovers countless horizons that are yet to appear.

By following the course of the psychic life of one woman here, another there, one can little by little open up paths in the vigorous green continent of femininity on its own terrain, respecting its saliences, reliefs and characteristics, which will appear as invariants.

I think that the investigation of "femininity" based on its evolution during the life of a woman may represent a reversal in the way this topic has been approached, getting away from the weight of classical theories that have been forged on the basis of what is "masculine," and on female pathologies.

This is the condition for this exploration: to run the risk of undertaking it from the point of view of its own course, adding to the baggage only a few relevant theories that were evoked during this experience giving it some meaning.

The evolution of a girl

This case description starts off with observations of a mother–daughter relationship—from pregnancy until the age of two-and-a-half—followed by some meetings with the parents until the girl was eleven years old, at which time she began analysis with me, staying until she was sixteen.

I had already completed my training when I began these observations. Based, therefore, on a reasonable working-through of the Oedipus complex, I was able to provide a sufficient "internal setting" (Alizade, 2002) for the mother–baby pair, and establish a solid "field" for psychic listening (Baranger, 1961–1962). These factors have in common the space for a third person, the new, the unknown, opened up by the "place of the father" in the observer's or analyst's mind. It is an internal object that structures both the analyst's or observer's psychic apparatus and the listening that can be offered in the intersubjective situation.

Our purpose here is to show, through a clinical case, how moments in the structuring of "femininity" appear and are constituted in a girl's relationship with her mother, with support from her father (Haudenschild, 1994). I agree with Stoller (1968) that certain factors are always present in the particular way that each woman blossoms, or grows, including both *sexual* (biological and innate) and *generic* factors (related to behaviour and characteristics that are socially encouraged by family and culture, varying according to the child's sex).

Observation of the mother–baby relationship

The girl in her parents' mind

I have observed Bruna's relationship with her mother since pregnancy. Her parents were happy when they discovered that their child would be a girl. The father was pleased because he never had a sister, and the mother, because ever since she herself was small, she had wanted her first child to be a girl.

I talked with the mother about the observations I would like to carry out. She shows me the bedroom that has been prepared for Bruna (the name of her favourite doll when she was a child). She also informs me that she herself has one older sister, one younger sister, and a much younger brother, now only eleven years old: "My mother only has eyes for him", she tells me.

The father's family lives near the couple, he being the oldest of three brothers.

Bruna, age two days

The places the father gives to me and to the maternal grandmother

In the hospital room, only two days after Bruna was born, the father points to a place near the window for me. "From there you can see her little face very clearly", he says. When the baby is brought in, the maternal grandmother tries to hold her, but the father takes Bruna to the mother's breast for feeding. The grandmother then finds a more distant couch to sit on, and stays there.

Age nine days

The place the father gives the mother

The following week, I go to the maternal grandmother's house [she has been taking care of Bruna's mother after her release from the maternity hospital]. Bruna is also cared for by the grandmother, as precisely and as quickly as an express train. After bathing and dressing Bruna, the grandmother puts her in my arms and says she is going to get some juice for the mother. I take the baby over to the mother, who is lying on a couch in a dark corner, at the opposite end of the large living room. The mother then smiles radiantly, as she had when she received Bruna to feed the previous week, when I observed her for the first time at the hospital, under the father's watchful eye. I open the curtain a little and the morning sun shines in on the two of them.

I later realized that, like the father, I too took Bruna to her mother, so the latter could occupy her place of woman–mother. She thus was no longer a mere phallic extension of her own mother (Bruna's grandmother), but the individual mother of a particular baby. This time it was I who made the "cut", and Bruna's mother seemed grateful.

The "father's place" in the mother's mind

In the words of Bruna's maternal grandmother, the maternal grandfather is not very present. He travels constantly and leaves all the domestic decisions to his wife, who seems mechanical ("perfect", in her daughter's words), always busy with chores and very concerned with overprotecting her youngest son.

In my opinion the "place of the father" in Bruna's mother's mind is established little by little through her relationship with her husband and the husband's father, who appreciates her and his little granddaughter very much. My presence of attentive, but silent observation, in contrast to the over-protective "*doing*" of the perfect and idealized mother ("Ideal Ego", Freud, 1914), gradually makes room for the mother to develop her own way of "*being*". An internal object corresponding to the phallic mother (Freud, Klein)—an Ideal Object whose counterpart is an Ideal Ego, a rigid subject—slowly gives way to a comprehensive internal object (Bion, 1959).

With respect to the internalization of this object, I would like to highlight the mother's capacity for *reverie*, expressed as the capacity to take in, to accept, and patiently to give meaning to the baby's confusing projective identifications (Bion, 1962b). She can accept that her baby is different from her, and see it as someone new, not merely an extension of herself.

Only after this relationship is established can the child benefit from containment for its psychic life, and then represent it. Esther Bick (1968) gave the name of "psychic skin" to this self-containment, and stated that the real presence of the mother is necessary for it to be constituted. The child attains an organized consensuality on the basis of the mother's smell, the taste of the milk, and other tactile sensations, including her mother's voice and gaze (*common sense*, Bion, 1962b). The child goes beyond sensuality and is able to perceive the psychism of the mother who is caring for it. If this were not so (Haudenschild, 1997), the child would continue at the mercy of one or another reassuring sensory experience, such as a piece of cloth with tactile sensation and scent, to serve as "second skin", a sensory wrapping for its mental apparatus (Anzieu, 1985). However, the baby would not be able to root its sensory experiences in its mind, nor represent and retain them as emotional experiences.

Bruna seemed to enjoy a good relationship with her mother, supported by the father ("original unity"—Perez Sanchez & Abelio, 1980; Salas, 1974) and this allowed her to constitute her own mental containing, her own thoughts, her alpha function (Bion, 1962a,b).

Bruna happy to be a girl

Age twenty months

The pride of the pubis: "Look, I'm a woman!"

I observe Bruna in the dawn of her femininity, her left hand pressing a doll to her breast while she holds a transparent purse with make-up in her right hand. She goes over to her mother's sewing machine and sits on the pedal facing the wheel. Then she puts the doll and the bag behind her and asks me for the car keys I still have in my hand. [I have just arrived.] She "turns on" the car motor with the key and as she "steers" with the wheel under the machine, she sways on the pedal, very happy.

After a while I tell her she looks like her mother taking her for a ride in her car. She looks at me, gets up and comes over to me. She then lifts up her dress, pulls down her panties, and proudly shows me some little hairs drawn on her pubis with a pen. She contentedly seems to be saying, "I'm just like Mommy, in everything!" She then immediately goes back to her play.

My first reaction is one of surprise. After that I felt gratitude to Bruna for having shared her intimacy with me. Mother had left the room and we were alone. When she returns, I tell her that Bruna is taking her little daughter for a ride in the car. Then, to her mother's surprise, Bruna repeats the scene. "I can't believe it," the mother says. "She drew those hairs so well, without my noticing!"

It is interesting to note that Bruna reveals herself "as a woman" to me first. Bernstein (1990) says that the child needs another woman to show its individuation because, due to the projection of its symbiotic desires, it fears that the mother may not want to be separated from her. This author also says that a girl's evolution is more difficult than a boy's, because she has to separate herself from her mother and, at the same time, she depends on her mother for her identification as a woman. "Another woman" can facilitate this process. In this case, Bruna's paternal grandmother, who had no daughters, was also very helpful.

Bernstein (1990) refers to *specifically feminine anxieties* derived from the characteristics of the female genitals (anxieties related to *access, penetration,* and *diffusivity*), and the girl *tries to dominate these anxieties* through *externalization, concretization, regression,* and *dependence* on others. All these attempts, except regression, appear in the brief description given above: Bruna expressed her "being a woman" very concretely, under the gaze of "another woman", as she drove her daughter in a car, and carried a purse.

Age two-and-a-half

God–woman

Mother tells me that Bruna saw a beautiful cloud in the sky with an rainbow behind it, and asked her an unexpected question: "Isn't that God, Mother? That beautiful woman who lives over the clouds, who takes care of the world?" The mother was surprised at this correlation between God and woman, and asked me if I had ever heard a child talk like that.

I don't think even Melanie Klein had ever heard that kind of statement when she coined her concept of "phallic mother", a mother who has all power: the power to be impregnated, to bear children, give birth to new lives, nurture them, and even have the father's powerful penis inside her (Klein, 1932a). Bruna refers to a God–woman who is not phallic and powerful: she just takes care of the world, which is under her colourful and radiant protection.

My observations continued until Bruna was two-years-and-seven-months old, after which time her parents would only occasionally call on me for some counselling.

Conversations with the parents

"Among women" (age four)

> The mother, who by now also has a son, five-months-old, comes in for counselling about how she can talk with her daughter about sex. Bruna is always asking about her "froggy" (the name her mother calls the external genitals): "Does your froggy have that butter like mine does? Where does it come from? From inside? Does it come at night when I'm asleep?"

> In a drawing her mother shows me, Bruna has drawn herself and her mother, both naked. The external genitals are represented accurately, as is the long, parted hair on their heads, as if their sexuality were protected under their hair.

The trust Bruna shows talking openly with her mother is extraordinary (Keiser, 1953). It is also interesting that the mother has a name for women's external genitals, about which they can talk (Lerner, 1976; Alizade, 1992). Bruna's drawing shows that she feels protected under her mother's hair and thoughts, as well as under her own.

Oedipal anxieties (age seven)

Bruna's parents come to me one day to talk about their daughter's (and their own) anxieties. Her mother teaches at night, and the children stay with their father until mother arrives. Bruna plays with her father selling him her mother's "jewels" and he has to buy them for the mother in accordance with the daughter's instructions. Occasionally when her mother is late coming home, he puts her to bed, but she cries: "I want my mommy!" The father is very patient, but doesn't know exactly what do to.

Bisexual fantasies (age ten)

"Among men"

Bruna's mother tells me that her daughter enjoys doing some things that boys like and others that girls like. "She took tests with a female English ballet dancer, who praised her highly, but she also likes to play soccer with her cousins, who are all boys, as if she were one of them ..."

My feeling is that this freedom of being "among men" will help Bruna at school and in her professional and affective life. She will be able to transfer these positive experiences she has had with significant men (cousins, father, grandfather).

Bruna in analysis

Half-opened bud, half-closed rose,
a little bit of a girl, a little bit of a woman ...
[Machado de Assis, Girl and young lady, 1870]

At age eleven, Bruna begins analysis with me due to difficulties in adapting to a co-ed school she has been transferred to. She had always studied at an all-girls' school. According to her mother, the boys sometimes play rough practical jokes on the girls. They come up from behind, tie a scarf around a girl's waist and then pull her pants down. Even after being punished, they continue to surprise the girls. Bruna is always "terrified" just thinking about being the next victim.

Beginning of analysis (age eleven)

From top model to sexualized woman

At the beginning of analysis, Bruna designs and makes dresses with full skirts for her Barbie dolls, "as in grandma's times". She asks for my help, brings in patches of cloth and we organize a "fashion show". The mother tells me that Bruna has received some embroidered silk night gowns as a present from her grandmother. "She poses in front of the mirror in them. She looks just like a movie star". Barbie dolls do, undoubtedly, look like movie stars, as does Bob, who comes in a tuxedo. His role in the scene is to parade with each Barbie (like a classical male ballet dancer, who supports a ballerina). But one day, after having paraded with the "prettiest", Bob kisses her and takes off her clothes. Then she takes off his clothes, and they embrace, naked, in an improvised bed made with a paper napkin.

To distinguish herself from her mother, we observe Bruna adopting standards set by her paternal grandmother, whom Bruna sees as a model of grace and elegance, in contrast to her own mother and maternal grandmother. The paternal grandmother in this way serves as the "other" maternal figure for identification, with whom Bruna can work through her anxieties and efforts to master them in a less ambivalent way than with her mother.

Bruna blossoms (age twelve)

"For women"

Shortly before Christmas vacation, Bruna makes some flowers. She cuts off the leaves and petals and uses fine wire to shape them into small bouquets, to be given to her mother, grandmothers, aunts, and teachers. The "models" are the lilac, yellow, and pink roses in the garden outside my consulting room.

I tell her she is growing up, blossoming like the roses in my garden. That the space we have for our conversations, our analysis, is like fertile soil for her and that each rose is a little bit of her surfacing, opening up, coming into the light.

She laughs and adds: "It's easy (to make the bouquets), but if Marcelo (her art teacher) hadn't taught me how to hold and string the petals and make the peduncle, the roses wouldn't be very strong".

Bruna seems to realize the value of the support given by her father, the recognition from a man for a woman to blossom. It is like the peduncle of the rose, or like the setting for a jewel, without which it could not reflect the light. Bruna also seems to be talking about something like her fear of dispersion (Bernstein, 1990), of "losing her petals", if she does not have the internalized paternal firmness.

Embodied sensuality (age fourteen)

"For men"

During the week of her annual dance performance, Bruna dreams of "froggies" dancing on two legs, in a circle. She says that when she woke up she thought the dream was funny, very clear, with choreographic music.

I reminded her that "froggy" was the name she had given to her genitals when a child and she laughed pleasantly, adding that the dance was very sensual. She said "I'm even embarrassed to think of my father and grandfather watching it".

Bruna has the courage to show herself as a sexualized woman to male figures from her childhood. Will she be accepted?

Bruna's dreams

"Who are men? Who am I–woman?"

After the vacation Bruna no longer wants to play during her sessions. I invite her to lie down on the couch and she starts telling me her dreams.

The persecutory man (age fifteen)

The sound of a bull and the scent of a man

> I was with my classmates at school talking about our crushes. Suddenly

we heard a noise behind some bushes, like heavy breathing. I ran to the other side of the garden, up higher, and from there I saw a huge black bull. There was no danger where I was. I could see it and could run if I had to.

She associates the dream with a discussion when her mother told her father that with the smell of liquor on his breath (after he was out at a party with friends), she wouldn't sleep in the same bed with him. So her mother asked Bruna to trade places with her father, which she did. But the next day she told her mother she didn't want to do it any more because she didn't like the smell he had left on her pillow.

After a pause, Bruna comments that she is menstruating and that the smell bothers her greatly. "It's very strong." Can't you smell it?"

I tell her that she wonders if, besides her nice-smelling, rosy, girly part, I can accept her adult female sexuality and the fact that she is now able to reproduce.

Then she talks of her curiosity about men, their smells, their liquids, their phallic attributes. And especially about her fear of unexpected movements—not only of the bulls, but the movements inside her, toward them.

Anxieties of access, diffusivity, and penetration arise, as well as attempts to master them through regression, externalization, and dependence on the opinion of "another" woman, other than her mother.

Man (and woman) in search of their natural habitat

Now pretend I was your toy,
... your favorite pet.
Come, give me your hand: we are afraid no more. [Chico Buarque de Hollanda, in *John and Mary*, 1977]

The live adult bear

Three weeks later she dreams that:

Under my parents' bed, that was very high, there was a door, and a bear came out of it. It wasn't dangerous. It went up to the door, pushed

*it and left. I heard when it opened the front door of the house ... It was
like the teddy bear I've had for as long as I can remember, that's still in
my bedroom and still in perfect shape. It looks like a real bear. In the
dream it was as if it had grown up and was alive. It wasn't bad. It just
wanted to go out on the street. [Pause] What it really liked was the
forest and it didn't like having to sleep all locked up.*

I tell her that she seems to be talking about her own animal part that
accompanies her. Now that she is older, she feels imprisoned by her
parents (under the bed), who had always protected her. So she
wants to get out, get beyond the front door, to get to know her own
nature, to have contact with her "forest", her female nature. In the
past this nature had been brought to me as flowers, but today it
shows up as "forest", with wild flowers and wild animals—a
habitat for her femininity, just as the forest is the bear's habitat. But
if she is to move on she has to face risks. She doesn't know what she
will find, and she is sensitive to everything that goes on inside her,
including the bear's unforeseen footsteps.

She says she saw a movie about bears: "When the cubs are grown
up the mother climbs a tall tree and leaves the young bears up there.
They have to get down alone, and when they do, the mother is gone".

Now Bruna works through her curiosities and fears in relation to
men's (and her own) sexuality by replacing the bull by her fuzzy
little teddy bear, which serves as a transitional object (Winnicott,
1951, 1971). It has been with her all her life—an object that helped to
begin the separation from her mother.

Now the bear stands for the astonishing man and for the growing
femininity that is beginning to take on importance for her. It refers
not only to the integration of female sexuality, but also to psychic
bisexuality and the complementarity between man and woman.

Integrations of the self and of femininity

*On the eve of her farewell to analysis, to her parents' home, and to
her childhood (age sixteen)*

Green bows on the green tree

   I dreamed that Mario [her boyfriend] and I were visiting grandpa, who lived on the top floor, but he had gone out. We were taking care of some children, and a boy wanted to play outside, in the yard. We went down and I saw grandpa's car come in. I told Mario I would go up while he waited for the boy. When I went into grandpa's apartment he was trimming the Christmas tree. It was very alive and vigorous and strong, taller than a person. Grandpa had brought some green bows that were so beautiful that I thought anyone who wanted to could see them. He placed one of the bows on the tree and left a candy wrapper behind. That way the bow could be seen easily. When he saw me, I gave him such a tight hug! It hurt me to see that I'm almost his size. It's not like when I used to hug his legs. I thought: until when? He's so old ... "Grandpa, can I help you?" I asked. He didn't answer me, but let me help, like he did when my brother and I were little: He never refused our help. Then Mario came in with the children and everybody thought the tree was beautiful. That's the kind I want to have some day at my house.

(I remember the dream about the bear: it had gone out of the house, like Mario and the boy, who also *went down* from the top floor to the yard—like the way the bears get down out of the trees when they have grown up. In that dream, like in this one, she herself noticed what had gone on *inside* the house: in the couple's bedroom, in her grandfather's room. I, therefore, think she was noticing a difference between men's walking outside and women's walking inside, in the awareness and constitution of her sexual identity. But she also seemed to integrate these two paths inside herself, integrating her internal bisexuality, built up through the already internalized female and male identities.)

I tell her she has noticed how time has gone by and how she has grown up. Now she and Mario can take care of children themselves, as parents. And her grandfather has gotten old. On the eve of Christmas vacation and before her farewell, she wondered out loud: "How long?", meaning how long will her beloved grandfather, her parents, and myself be there for her? She already seems to have inside her this same living strength of the tree that her grandfather decorated with green bows, beautiful like femininity. It is not apparent, but it is there for anyone who wants to see it. (The shape and arrangement of the bows around the tree remind me of the "froggies" dancing in a circle, besides the clear association with the idea of close ties.)

She adds that: "He was proud that I was the little woman in the house".

Florence Guignard (1989, p. 1052) says that:

Once the adult biological capacities have developed, the integration of internal bisexuality gives new meaning to the primal scene, derived from the child's Oedipal organization ... in a mental space that is structured, from now on, both through the transgenerational vector of the parental function and through the generational vector of a loving relationship. [1989]

In her dream Bruna visits her grandfather as "Mario's girlfriend". Since the grandmother is not present, she herself makes a "pair" with her grandfather, who accepts her help in decorating the tree. But now she is not afraid to be confused with his wife, as she had feared with her father when she was seven and he stayed at home at night with her. The grandfather's body serves as a reference for her body, now grown up and adult. The climate is not of fear of being invaded, but of mourning because a farewell is approaching that cannot be avoided, a farewell to her childhood figures. In an instant, Bruna understands the inexorable difference among the four generations: grandparents, parents, she herself, and her children.

And she happily remembers her grandfather's pride in her being "a little woman".

The "green continent"

This pride in being a woman, internalized by Bruna, can give her what Lou Andreas Salome called the narcissistic "lack of pride", described as the healthy narcissistic pleasure of a person who has an internal gift that is almost imperceptible, but beautiful, like the green bows.

Those who have eyes to see, can see them.

And if the interiority is better revealed (cf. M. Klein) as a symbolistic poem—where the image produces its own shape (Mitchell, 1986)—than as a myth as Freud suggested, the analyst's poetic sensitivity to the images being produced, session after session, can (or maybe cannot) distinguish them as "selected facts" (Bion, 1962b), full of meaning.

Some of these images, revealers of a woman's interiority, have taken shape in this text. I hope they can continue to be unveiled (Haudenschild, 1999) on the basis of their repercussions on the mental life of each reader, and at the unpredictable moment of each reading. This moment may be like the intertwining of numerous stories, woven by various generations, like the highways that criss-cross a continent.

Our "green continent" still has few roads, but they are promising, as they criss-cross through the green outside, the green inside . . .

Note

1. My gratitude to my colleague Daniela Sitzer who revised this paper.

CHAPTER NINE

A clandestine identity:
pathways of contemporary femininity[1]

Emma Piccioli and Giangaetano Bartolomei

I t is generally agreed that the psychoanalytic theory on femininity is an essential part of the general theory on psychosexual development to the extent that they stand or fall together. However, a quick perusal of the relative literature leaves us with the impression of, on the one hand, a labyrinth of pathways that are fascinating but lead nowhere and, on the other hand, of controversies without a solution. Discussions on the theme have been so charged with emotion as to obscure the existence of methodological and theoretical problems beyond, for example, the opposing theses on female masochism or the primary or defensive nature of penis envy. Even the literature that attempts a revision of Freud's theory on female psychosexual development has added to these misunderstandings and ambiguities by declaring many concepts to be outdated, but without drawing from them any consequences regarding the theory on psychosexual development as a whole, whether male or female.

A consequence of this state of affairs, as anyone investigating the theme soon realizes, is that there is a difference between the theory on women and women as they really are. We, too, have had this sensation when our women patients presented us with their "enigmas", certainly, but also with the force, the insistence and the incisiveness that every patient places on his or her need to be listened to. In the face of these concrete experiences, the woman as she is described in the theory receded, like the mythical creature of a continent that is, if not dark then at least grey and confused. In the theory, the woman of our clinical experience seemed to no longer exist, and we were led to think of the "feminine" of the theory as being a residual category including all that is shadowy and disquieting (and perhaps even unknowable) in the human mind. It is almost as though this representation of femininity, typical of mythology, had continued into psychoanalytic theory, rendering it, too, obscure and incomprehensible.

On the more crucial points of the psychoanalytic debate, Grossman (1976, p. 302) supports the equidistance between the theses in conflict, so that "the reasons for controversy" become the object of the investigation. He states that taking any stand whatsoever on the contents would contribute either to perpetuating the old mythology or to constructing a new one. But we should like to add that even without taking a stand, one cannot ignore the fact that in this debate, the different and sometimes conflicting prejudices, ideals, and values of Western culture come into play, either openly or surreptitiously, both in the theory as well as in clinical practice. Thus, a study of the psychoanalytic literature on women and on femininity will provide us with information about the historical change in psychoanalytic thought, about how it is connected with all the other social processes and forms part of a totality that is in evolution. It tells us of the ideological (in the original, strict sense of the word) character of psychoanalytic anthropology, analogous to every other global representation of the human being, of his nature, his mind, his destiny.

The different way in which we, compared with Freud, consider the question of femininity today, or even our refusal to consider it at all in his terms, is the consequence of a historic global change involving the thing itself and not only its concept: that is, the Western or westernized woman. There has been a profound modification, on the one hand—and it is ground for bitter conflict—in what women do, what they think they can do, what they expect of themselves; and on the other hand, in what the social environment expects them to do or not to do. In brief, what women are in their own eyes and in the eyes of those who observe them has changed; and many of the cultural presuppositions of the traditional feminine mythology have been weakened. Although when Freud was writing, the mystery or enigma of femininity still prevailed (Freud, 1933)—and not only in psychoanalytic theory— today these expressions sound outmoded, also because we are always less willing to suppose that unfathomable mysteries still exist in ourselves or in the world surrounding us. Even those who admit the extreme possibility that there is no predetermined femininity (or masculinity), should also admit that the question cannot be decided in the feminine sense alone by invoking the need to review only the theory regarding the psychosexual development of the woman.

Freud's reflections on femininity are, in any case, vindicated by the many contradictions attributed to them for placing the origin of the denominator common to all women on *a common experience* of the little girl comparing her own anatomy with that of little boys. Although, today, there is considerable doubt as to whether this event could be so fundamental for feminine identity, it is true that Freud, by appealing to a *psychic* event, annexes his question, "What is a woman and how is she produced?", entirely to psychoanalysis. In this way he distances himself from those formulations, of a biological or cultural nature, that explain a hypothetical female psychology on the basis of biological or cultural factors alone; and he identifies its root not in an objective fact, but in the subjective experience produced by its perception: the anatomy of the woman is her destiny (Freud, 1912, 1924a) because it determines *a lived experience, endowed with meaning*. This latter is indeed a tributary of cultural factors inasmuch as "the awareness of the difference" can produce the "Freudian woman" only if the penis has the value of phallus. But is the evaluation of the penis as phallus an intrinsic psychic necessity, a kind of human universal present in all cultures, or is it a cultural correlation of a historic (and as such perishable, although almost universal) modality of the organization of human cohabitation and of social definition of the relationship between the sexes? And in the Freudian discourse, how much space is there for assuming that cultural factors have contributed to the construction of personality structure? Very little space, it would appear. In fact, when Freud evokes the social conditioning of psychosexual development (and he does this often), he refers to the traditional paradigm of a non-social human nature that submits to social necessities during the course of educational processes, and he thinks only marginally of cultural differences as determining different developmental outcomes.

For our part, we have attempted to gather observations and reflections resulting from clinical experience on the theme of femininity and its biological–cultural connections, although we are aware that it is a fragmentary work or, rather, fragments of a possible work, held together by certain guiding interests. In our study, there are two points of view that converge, diverge, and sometimes clash, and from which it is possible to examine the questions we raise. One is both theoretical and clinical and is centred on a consideration of the psychic processes as being natural and unvarying; the other is historical–social and centres on the variety and changes in the mental world in relation to the differences between cultures and to the way in which a culture changes with time.

The basic question that inspired our reflections was this: for an individual who is genetically and anatomically feminine, what does it mean to be psychically feminine? And how is this produced?

The models of research that, through clinical–observational and experimental methods, have defined the concept of gender identity and its production, both in the male as well as in the female, refer to several authors, but it was Stoller (1968, 1976, 1979), in particular, who integrated the experimental results with the data gathered during a long period of clinical practice, much of which was conducted with intersexual subjects. Stoller's conclusions indicate that the feeling of belonging to a gender (whether masculine or feminine) is already in operation during the very first years of life, and is determined by inborn factors (genetic, hormonal, central) as well as by acquired factors. These latter depend on the social designation that takes place at birth, as well as on learning and on early identificatory vicissitudes, and they therefore operate in the relational spheres. Maternal cognition ("This is my baby boy/baby girl") is determinant for the formation of gender identity.

Stoller postulates the idea of *nuclear* gender identity to describe a primary state that in no way implicates either the role or the object relations, and from which will derive the wider notion of gender identity. For Stoller, the terms "masculinity" and "femininity" do not have biological connotations even though they may have biological roots, and they refer to the *feeling of self* (identity) and to how this feeling defines the role. In this way Stoller believes that he has avoided the biological type of equation: masculine = activity, feminine = passivity. He says: "... femininity is what a person and her (or his) parents, peers, and society agree is femininity; the criteria change from place to place and time to time" (1979, p. 40). It seems to us that this definition authorizes us to expand our initial question as follows: in this place and age, what are the generally agreed characteristics of femininity (and of masculinity)? Today, what can a woman reasonably expect to be able to do and to be, and what does the social environment expect of her? What are women in their own eyes and in the eyes of those who observe them?

Project and ideality

The patients who have led us to reflect on these issues are women who, although they have reached important maturational stages and a good organization of the self, reveal in different ways a mixture of guilt feelings and of illegitimacy when carrying out projects of their own outside of traditional patterns (e.g. maternity). Judging from our experience, it seemed to us that this difficulty was, in the analytic world, characteristically if not exclusively feminine, inasmuch as men may display a feeling of incapability or of insufficiency regarding their own projectuality, but not of illegitimacy in cultivating it. It has been interesting for us to explore this problem in relation to the more general problem of feminine identity including gender identity, personal identity, and the public (or social) aspect of the latter.

The women we are talking about are intelligent, very sensitive, with good relational capacities. In spite of this they describe themselves as being incapable and they are unable to perceive their own personal worth; on the other hand, they idealize their husbands or companions. The analyst seems to be the only one who is aware of their capacities as well as of the insufficiencies of their partners. In fact, there is a very evident splitting, in that their discourse evokes in the analyst the image of an inadequate partner while their words go in the opposite direction. The analyst thus finds herself listening to two irreconcilable discourses that seem to spring from two different levels of awareness: one expressing the feelings of self-devaluation and of idealization of the partner; the other the perception of his negative characteristics and of their own talents. This second discourse takes place almost imperceptibly, as though it were an attempt at partial concealment or camouflaging, not very far from awareness. But every interpretation aimed at confronting the patients with their capable reality is received with surprise and often with panic. For these women, accepting their own capabilities seems to be extremely dangerous and subject to a very powerful interdiction.

When they think of some form of self-affirmation and self-realization, these very talented women are prey to painful feelings of guilt and illegitimacy, as though usurping a role to which they are not entitled. They give the impression of withdrawing in fright before any project of self-realization because they feel it as being equivalent to "too much"—that it is in some way blameful and dangerous. They can even feel that it is "too much" to have a space and a time for themselves, free from the role that they often fill as helpers to the whole family, their friends, etc. Their motto (for the purpose of concealing important aspects of the self) could be: "This is good enough for me", as though they could not allow themselves to be visible, even in their own eyes. How many unused driving licences, how many dreams in which precious identity documents are lost or allowed to expire! It is forbidden and illegitimate to "occupy a space", "ask for things", "object to something", "be strong", "be capable, be different", "compare oneself" with others, if it would be to one's own advantage. Love is seen as being a sacrifice implying the question/request: "how much have you renounced as a sign of love?".

A., for example, has given up the apartment she owns and has left it to her boyfriend with whom, what is more, she is on bad terms. She lives the life of a vagabond, staying sometimes with her mother, sometimes with friends; she has dispossessed herself of her own home. She says: "If I am strong, then I am unable to love ...", and:

"If I ask, it means that I am here, I make myself heard, I make a choice ... there are consequences".

And B. says: "I'd rather make a mistake than do something right that makes me visible ... If things go well, I get frightened, my relationships with the others can change. Sooner or later I have to make myself stupid and dull. Only as a mother can I allow myself to assert myself, to be different".

Strangely enough, for these women the aspect of identity that traditionally sums up femininity, i.e. maternity, on the whole does not appear to be compromised.

Another common characteristic is the idealization of the father, who is often a figure of success. Only rarely do these patients express perplexity (but never very critical) regarding the lack of paternal support of their public achievement, i.e. in spheres other than that of maternity. As far as the maternal imago is concerned, their mothers are often described as being dissatisfied, observant of their duties, but joyless and unable to play.

In our patients the feeling of self appears to be painfully impaired and weighed down with a combination of impotence, illegitimacy, shame, and anger. As well as a wound, a conflict is also in operation between what these women would like to be (or are) and what they think they should be and/or will allow themselves to be. We thought we could conceptualize their condition by relating it to a kind of anguish regarding their ideal projectuality, using here the two meanings of the word "anguish" (i.e. suffocating narrowness, distress).

When we think of an existential project, we refer specifically to an "identificatory projectuality"—the natural drive towards growing up that constitutes, together, "a hope, a promise and a maturational impulse" (Chasseguet-Smirgel, 1985). As it is described in the literature, the maturational project of the boy child has an apparent linearity: it is his hope of growing up to be like his father, of doing things that grown men do. Freud already refers to a maturational ideal in "Creative writers and day-dreaming" (1908 [1907]) when he speaks about the little boy's wish to grow up being expressed in his games, but it is only in his work of 1914 ("On narcissism") that he introduces the concept of Ideal Ego. At the beginning, states Freud, what the boy projects before himself is his own narcissism: he himself is his own ideal. Subsequently, he will entrust this ideal to his own homosexual object, the father. At the same time he will have to disidentify himself from his first object, the mother, in order to consolidate his own masculinity (Greenson, 1968).

In an attempt to account for the situation of our patients described above, we wonder: To whom does the little girl entrust *her* identificatory project? What can *she* project before herself as her own maturational ideal?

Two different theses on the maturational project of the little girl merit a brief comparison. According to Greenson (*ibid*.): "The girl, too, must disidentify from mother if she is to develop her own unique sense of self, but her identification with mother *helps* her to establish her femininity". Many authors are in agreement with this thesis. Others, on the contrary, including Argentieri in Italy, do not accept the concept of a *primary identification* with the mother as the basis for gender identity, but believe that the identification able to promote it cannot be primary because it presupposes two important maturational steps: separation from the mother, and distinction between mother-object and father-object (between male and female). Instead, at the primary level, there would be an undifferentiated fusional situation, the potential substratum of only an imitative pseudo-femininity. Furthermore, growing up and becoming a woman (i.e. corporeally the same as the mother) could, for the girl, assume the meaning of being the mother, thus plunging her back into the primal fusional bond that prevents the establishment of identity (Argentieri, 1985, 1988). In order to be independent, today's women must, therefore, be able to disidentify with the mother through the same modalities that are essential for masculine development (Bernstein, 1983). The ideal objects that orient the identification and identity pathways for the girl will thus be both maternal and paternal in her case also, and must help her to bring about an integration between a characteristically maternal gender and a personal ideal that cannot be anything but paternal. At this point a conflict arises in that the girl must contemporaneously remain linked to her mother by a common *gender identity* as well as differentiate herself from her for her own *personal identity*, based precisely on the *difference* (characterized as masculine).

A clinical example allows us to further investigate our points of view.

C. has given up her own university career in favour of that of her husband, and for many years she has been his ghost-writer. She tells the analyst that this role suits her because it is her husband who "has the ideas" and is creative. C.'s opinion of herself is that she is inadequate as a wife, mother, and scholar. The analyst, on the other hand, has learned to appreciate the intelligence, culture, and sensitivity of this woman who anonymously writes scientific books for her husband.

During the course of the analysis, C. very rapidly appropriates her maternal capacities and establishes an excellent relationship with her children, finally recognizing her value as a mother. However, this remains separate from her self-devaluation in other fields.

When describing how she viewed her parents when she was a child, C. expresses the dilemma present in her identificatory projectuality: "On one side there was a person, good-looking, tall, who goes out into the world, he is important. On the other side there was a person who takes care of you, makes you do your homework, looks after you, but who always has a headache and doesn't seem to enjoy herself. But the one who goes out into the world, while on one hand he thought I was pretty and clever ... everyone said I looked like him ... on the other hand he did everything he could to stop me from going out into the world, threatening that he wouldn't love me any more. Esteem, yes, pride and permission to look like him; just as long as he could control everything. My place was inside. Making my mother angry was to risk concrete things like slaps and scolding. Making him angry was like losing the sun, a question of life or death".

To escape from the interdiction, C. tries to get away through a form of creativity and self-assertion that is hidden and almost clandestine (ghost-writer), inasmuch as the danger lies not so much in resembling her father as in making visible both the resemblance and her own masculine expressive capacity, in confirming her own autonomous existence as an individual endowed with masculine strength. But what is the nature of the interdiction that has condemned her to the anguish of the "place inside"? How and at what levels does it operate? What is the danger that C., within herself, tries to exorcize by renouncing her masculine ideal of liberty?

The conflict is between the ego and its ideal. In order to develop, the ego ideal needs an environment that welcomes the child's accomplishments by offering her satisfactory narcissistic confirmation, while at the same time imposing on her sufficient frustrations so that the character of ideality as driving force and promise is not lost. A certain amount of pressure on the part of the object is also essential, tending to direct the subject towards development while satisfying passive-receptive needs (Fain & Marty, 1959). In the relationship between C. and her ideal object, these conditions seem to have been met only up to a certain point. From a genetic viewpoint, one would say that C. has been the victim of a tyrannical event and that she fears losing its love and protection if she does not submit to it.

If one interprets the material from the point of view of *function*, then the father who "goes out into the world" represents an aspect of knowledge as well as independence and assertiveness (all active aims). The interdiction therefore strikes at a level implying, in a broad sense, the development of separateness and the drive towards knowledge and expanding the confines of the self, and this is what the patient is aiming at. But represented in this way, and with the sexual difference, if the patient were to follow her aim she would expose herself to the evaluation of her own phallicism both of theory and environment. She *therefore defensively* adopts the thesis of phallic monism.

A clandestine identity

During the recuperation of her own symbolic space, when finally a room for herself is ready, one day C. tells that at least from the time of her adolescence she has imagined herself as being "a lanky boy", inherited from the heroes of her youth such as Ivanhoe, Huckleberry Finn, the pirate chief, etc. The lanky boy "is something that has to do with adolescence, when you are exploring, you walk about, you are restless, sometimes you manage to follow a road. But I always had to remain there, passively waiting for a fairy prince to arrive". She continued: "The lanky boy is free ... but I have to be careful what I do, not to speak too loudly ... he lives to search for things, he is someone who searches, thinks, walks ..., he can do one thing and then another, it comes naturally to him".

C. presents this internal character to the analyst hesitatingly, with the clearly expressed fear that it might be judged a deviance (the guilty phallicism of the theory). In this way she also signals a fundamental aspect of her identity, although it has never emerged. The lanky boy who "can do one thing and then another" represents an alternative to the identificatory dilemma that is paralysing the formation of her independent projectuality.

The appearance of this character in C.'s analysis suggests that at a certain moment the analytic process has favoured the (re)formation of the patient's intuition of what she *could be*. A "boy", therefore, also expressed as a *possibility for the future* solicited by the project of an analyst who does not exclude from her mind the possibility that the patient (a woman) could legitimately aspire to identity aspects that are transgressive compared with those conceded to the Freudian woman—a possibility that the analyst derives from her own theories on feminine (and masculine) identity and her own system of values.

The resumption within the analysis of a natural maturational trend constitutes one of the qualities of the ideal ego that would supply even very problematic patients with an intuitive awareness of how they could be; an awareness that would support them by supplying them, during the course of the analysis, with a kind of deep understanding of the steps that will lead them to become what they are (Chasseguet-Smirgel, 1985).

The theoretic difficulties apparent at this point concern the notions of activity/passivity and of guilt, and their placement within the modern theory on femininity and identification mechanisms. Regarding the problem of guilt (feminine), positions vary according to the theoretic model of reference. Some analysts agree in defining the question in relation to the father and his idealization (rather than to the mother) and they locate the theoretic connections in the opposites of activity/passivity.

Chasseguet-Smirgel (1985a) speaks of a type of guilt that is specifically feminine and is linked to the change of object and to the idealization process underlying this developmental moment. The latter implies an instinctual defusion by which the object-mother is invested only negatively and the object-father only positively, and consequently the little girl tends to repress and counter-invest her own aggressive feelings towards the father. This results in a feeling of guilt that is specifically feminine and is connected with the sadistic–anal component when it refers to aggressiveness, linked both to incorporation and to the assertiveness necessary for social success. Chasseguet also observes that it is reductive to link feminine conflictuality exclusively to the internal mother of early infancy and includes in her considerations the contribution made by external factors to the reinforcement of guilt feelings in women. Among these factors should be included those deriving from a theory that interprets the feminine desire for success as a masculine protest linked to penis envy that, in its turn, can arouse profound feelings of guilt. Feminine desire, Chasseguet points out, is not that of becoming a male, but of becoming an independent woman.

The main obstacle to achieving this state lies in the defensive operation of identifying independence with a partial object—the paternal phallus (phallic identification). This would account for what can generally be defined as female masochism, in that one of the characteristics of this condition is the offering of oneself as the object of the other. Thus, through the offer of herself, the little girl safeguards the father who then loves her and protects her from the mother, even at the cost of permanent dependence. If one were to adhere to this clear and coherent line of thought, the problems of our patients would be resolved, and the anguish of the "place inside" could be considered, above all, as the expression of an undifferentiating anal defence operation. Although this may well provide a reason for unconscious fantasy, it does not deal with the identificatory dilemma that arises especially during adolescence, when it is necessary to re-experiment and reformulate infantile experiences in order to be able to constitute oneself as a subject or an ego, and to compare and connect this personal identity with its *social* correspondent. It is generally considered that this process of identity construction (especially in girls) is completed when the child has assumed the gender identity of the mother and replicates her social roles, while not sufficient importance is given to the question regarding the *pathways* along which the little girl will construct her own personal identity as a woman, and that will make of her, as of each one of us, a unique and unrepeatable individual who exists according to a project of self that gives meaning to her being. From this point of view, the idea of *active* feminine sexual desire, introduced by Chasseguet-Smirgel in her work, should be reconsidered and elaborated with reference to those identifications pertaining specifically to the adolescent period.

In his work on narcissism, Freud distinguishes two modalities of object choice—narcissistic and anaclitic. He describes various feminine typologies of both these modalities. The most widespread feminine type (also the most quoted, especially by critics of Freud's theories on femininity) loves exclusively narcissistically. Then, there is a variant of the narcissistic modality, in which the passage to object love becomes possible through maternity; this type of woman would be able to love her own child as other than herself and would thus experience object love. Lastly, Freud describes a third type of women: "... they still retain the capacity of longing for a masculine ideal—an ideal which is in fact a survival of the boyish nature that they themselves once possessed" (Freud, 1914, p. 90). From a viewpoint different from that of Freud (that is at the basis of the typology just mentioned), our patients appear to have reached that stage of development that allows for the establishment of object love relations, but they have had to relegate to clandestinity their masculine ideal self in order to allow it a possibility of survival.

The boy, who is the masculine ideal of C.'s adolescence, represents her wish for separateness, also in the sense of a possibility for self-affirmation and independent projectuality, with the implicit recognition of her right to experiment different pathways ("he can do one thing, and then another") and to freely explore, unburdened by pre-constituted interdictions. It is, therefore, important not to be misled by the manifest sexual identity of this personage who, through the fact that he is lanky and searches for things, expresses an attempt, regardless of gender (also evidenced by the androgenous adolescent characteristics), to constitute a personal identity that is independent and differentiated in respect to the identifications with the parental figures of infancy.

At a manifest level, and on the socio-cultural side of identity, the conflict that paralyses this type of woman lies in the unreconcilability of independence and dependence. They attempt a compromise by developing a clandestine creativity that, although it protects them from taking full responsibility, does not allow them the autonomy of movement in the outside world that is inherent in running the risks of life as though it were a wager. Again at a manifest level, the compulsory oblateness in the expression "this is good enough for me" appears in many ways to be a screen, as if they were hiding behind the other, dedicating themselves to him for fear of a self-assertive life that, amongst other things, could imply the loss of the illusion of being protected by their partner (an illusion also shared by the partner himself). These patients, therefore, fear losing the only possibility they have of expressing an aspect of their identity that they think can be allowed: their secret power over a partner who is, in fact, quite dependent on them for his own affirmation in the world; in other words, a function of *"eminence grise"*. In this sense, the oblateness could be considered as the assumption of a negative identity in order to better camouflage themselves and thus be able to express their protest and anger.

Furthermore, the fact that the "boy" is an adolescent also indicates the developmental stage at which the blockage has occurred. As Novelletto notes, one of the typical phenomena of this period of development is the rearrangement of the ideal ego. During adolescence, the parental idealizations that had resulted in the constitution of the ideal ego, in normal conditions undergo a brusque arrest "and the need for a new ideal ego becomes urgent" (Novelletto, 1991). C.'s new ideal has given up the character of the pirate chief, but it contains his spirit of adventure and of transgression (typical of adolescence). However, it becomes mitigated and integrated in the version of the lanky boy who, through his obvious androgeny, has been purified of characteristics that are too instinctual.

The inhibition to development of this ideal ego that, inasmuch as it characterizes the "difference", signals the constitution of a sentiment of personal identity, is expressed by C. through the representation of a mother who wants her to be "inside the house" *like her, and of a father who wants her to be "inside the house" unlike him.* It is as if he were saying to her: "You can not/must not do as I do". If she obeys, she keeps paternal approval and remains "his little girl", but she loses herself. If she disobeys, she asserts herself, but finds herself in a particular, specific type of psychic distress between admiration for the father and the pain of not seeing him accept the practical and vital consequences of this admiration; she feels resentment towards him, made up of heart-rending love. The idealized father thus becomes a persecutory and threatening object for her integrity ("making him angry was like losing the sun, a question of life or death"). It is rather like the equally awkward and painful situation of the little boy who, while trying to imitate the adult behaviour that he admires in his father, feels that the father reproaches him for his admiring imitation. But there is a substantial difference in the nature of the interdiction. In the case of the little boy, it is as though he were being told: "You are young: you can not/must not do as I do"; while the little girl is told: "You are a girl: you can not/must not do as I do". And so, while the boy is promised that one day, when he is grown up, he will be able to do as his father does, the little girl is denied every hope and every project in this direction, thus contributing to the formation of the condition we have described before as "anguish of the ideal ego".

There is no doubt that, as far as gender identity is concerned, psychoanalysts differ in the importance that they attach to certain notions compared with others. We may ask: Would it be possible for one analyst—in contrast to another—to cultivate in his or her own mind a fantasy-project such as the one we have described in the case of C.? What factors would this depend on? Certainly on many factors, not least of them being the system or the hierarchy of values to which the analyst adheres. And it is probably these values that lead an analyst to reject the Freudian woman as a model and to seek for a theory that is more congruent with these values.

But when we speak of values we enter into the realm of a *culture*, inasmuch as values are always the shared expression of a culture (roughly definable as a system of norms, values and models of behaviour). However, Western society, from the time of the crisis of cultural unity in the Middle Ages, has been characterized by the co-presence of systems of different, competitive, and conflicting values that are continually changing. This condition (that has been worsening in the last hundred years) cannot be overlooked when examining those aspects of psychoanalytic theory that are more closely connected to the socially shared representations of what is desirable or undesirable in human behaviour.

In conclusion, the fact that the feminine reality of our experience is so detached from the psychoanalytic theory that we spoke about at the beginning is, unfortunately, not merely speculative. If, through incapacity or unwillingness, we ignore the changes that have occurred in social and scientific reality, we overburden, sometimes to the limit of irretrievability, the delicate mechanism of the transference–counter-transference interplay (Wallerstein, 1973). This is particularly evident in the psychoanalytic treatment of women—a field in which many stereotypes have changed and where there has been a great increase in scientific–observational knowledge.

During the decline (at least in the Western or westernized world) of the rigid and often mortifying allocation and destination of male and female roles, a space has been created for greater freedom of action and scientific research on the theme, but a sensation of bewilderment is frequently felt by the men and women as well as by the research workers who are trying to study them. Unfortunately, this is the price that has to be paid when we abandon the shores of known—and perhaps false—certainties.

Summary

Beginning with an observation about the difference between psychoanalytic theory on women and the real women of their experience, the authors examine certain possible consequences of this state of affairs with reference to the anthropological status of psychoanalysis, and to those forms of identification pathology to which they are correlated on the clinical side. They point out how a study of psychoanalytic theory on femininity leads to an awareness of the historic change that has taken place in psychoanalytic thought and of its links with other social processes. Through clinical examples, they illustrate connections and divergences between gender identity, personal identity, and social identity in women, and the processes of their formation through an identificatory projectuality that, in the same way as in masculine development, involves the paternal functions as well.

Note

1. "A clandestine identity: pathways of contemporary femininity" by Emma Piccioli and Giangaetano Bartolomei was first published in Italian in *Rivista di Psicoanalisi*, Vol. 42, No. 1, 1996.

REFERENCES

Alizade, A. M. (1992). *Feminine Sensuality*. London: Karnac Books.
Alizade, A. M. (2002). El encuadre interno: nuevas aportaciones. Meeting APA-SPP, Paris, February.
Amati Mehler, J. (1992). Love and male impotence. *International Journal of Psycho-Analysis, 73*(3): 467–480.
Amati, J., Argentieri, S., & Canestri, J. (1990). *La Babele Dell'inconscio. Lingua Madre e Lingue Straniere Nella Dimensione Psicoanalitica* (Chapter 4). Milano: R. Cortina Editore.
Anzieu, D. (1985). *Le Moi-Peau*. Bordas: Paris.
Apfel, R. J., & Keylor, R. G. (2002). Psychoanalysis and infertility: myths and realities. *International Journal of Psychoanalysis, 83*: 85–104.
Argentieri, S. (1982). Sui processi mentali precoci dell'identità femminile. *Rivista di Psicoanalisi, 27*. Roma: Il Pensiero Scientifico Editore.
Argentieri, S. (1985). Sulla cosiddetta disidentificazione dalla madre. *Rivista di Psicoanalisi, 31*: 397–403.
Argentieri, S. (1988). Il sesso degli angeli. In: *Il Genere Sessuale*. Roma: Borla Editore.
Argentieri, S. (1992). Anna Freud, la figlia. In: *Psicoanalisi al Femminile*. Bari, Laterza: Vegetti Finzi.
Arlow, J. A. (1984). Disturbances of the sense of time—with special reference to the experience of timelessness. *Psychoanalytic Quarterly, 53*: 13–37.

Assis, M. (1870). Falenas. In: *Obras Completas, Volume III*. Rio de Janeiro: Aguillar, 1962.

Balsam, R. H. (1996). The pregnant mother and the body image of the daughter. *Journal of the American Psychoanalytic Association*, 44(suppl.): 401–427.

Baranger, M.y W. (1961–1962). La situación analítica como campo dinámico. In: *Problemas del Campo Analítico*. Buenos Aires: Kargieman.

Barrio Tarnawiecki, S. (1993). Reflexiones sobre la masculinidad. *Revista Pretextos*, 5: 123–139.

Bassin, D., Honey, M., & Kaplan, M. M. (Eds.) (1994). *Representations of Motherhood*. New Haven, CT: Yale University Press.

Benedek, T. (1956). Psychobiological aspects of mothering. *American Journal of Orthopsychiatry*, 26: 272–278.

Benedek, T. (1959). Parenthood as a developmental phase. *Journal of the American Psychoanalytic Association*, 7: 389–417.

Benedek, T. (1960). The organization of the reproductive drive. *International Journal of Psycho-Analysis*, 41: 1–15.

Bergmann, M. V. (1985). The effect of role reversal on delayed marriage and maternity. *Psychoanalytic Study of the Child*, 40: 197–219.

Bernstein, D. (1983). The female superego: a different perspective. *International Journal of Psycho-Analysis*, 64: 187–202.

Bernstein, D. (1990). Female genital anxieties, conflicts and typical mastery modes, *International Journal of Psycho-Analysis*, 71, 151–167.

Bibring, G. (1959). Some considerations of the psychobiological processes in pregnancy. *Psychoanalytic Study of the Child*, 14: 113–121.

Bibring, G., Dwyer, T., Huntington, D., & Valenstein, A. (1961). A study of the psychological processes in pregnancy and of the earliest mother–child relationship. *Psychoanalytic Study of the Child*, 16: 9–72.

Bick, E. (1968). The experience of the skin in early object-relations. *Int. J. Psychoanal.*, 49(2/3): 484–486.

Bion, W. (1959). Attacks on linking. In: *Second Thoughts*. London: Heinemann, 1967.

Bion, W. (1962a). A theory of thinking. In: *Second Thoughts*. London: Heinemann, 1967.

Bion, W. (1962b). *Learning from Experience*. London: Karnac, 1984.

Blum, D. (1997). *Sex on the Brain*. London: Penguin Books.

Brown, N. O. (1959). *Life Against Death*. New York: Vintage.

Buechler, S. (1999). Searching for a passionate neutrality. *Contemporary Psychoanalysis*, 35: 213–227.

Carter, R. (2000). *Mapping the Mind*. London: Phoenix.

Chasseguet-Smirgel, J. (1964). La culpabilité féminine. In: *Recherches Psychanalytiques Nouvelles sur la Sexualité Féminine*. Paris: PUF.

Chasseguet-Smirgel, J. (1985a). *Female Sexuality. New Psychoanalytic Views*. London: Karnac Books.

Chasseguet-Smirgel, J. (1985b). *Creativity and Perversion*. London: Free Association Books.

Chasseguet-Smirgel, J. (1985). *The Ego Ideal: A Psychoanalytic Essay on the Malady of the Ideal*. London: Free Association Books.

Chasseguet-Smirgel, J. (1986). *Sexuality and Mind. The Roles of the Father and the Mother in the Psyche*. New York and London: New York University Press.

Chodorow, N. J. (1978). *The Reproduction of Mothering* (2nd edn. with a new preface). Berkeley and Los Angeles: University of California Press.

Chodorow, N. J. (1999a). *The Power of Feelings: Personal Meaning in Psychoanalysis, Gender, and Culture*. New Haven, CT: Yale University Press.

Chodorow, N. J. (1999b). Preface to 2nd edn. In: *The Reproduction of Mothering* (*op. cit.*).

Cooper, S. H. (2000). *Objects of Hope: Exploring Possibility and Limit in Psychoanalysis*. Hillsdale, NJ: The Analytic Press.

Counut-Janin, M. (1998). *Féminin et Féminité*. Paris: Presses Universitaires de France.

Davidson, R. J., & Fox, N. A. (1982). Asymmetrical brain activity discriminates between positive and negative affective stimuli in human infants. *Science, 218*: 1235–1237.

De Marneffe, D. (n.d.). The desire to mother: its misinterpretation in psychoanalysis, feminism, and culture. Presented at Meetings of the American Psychoanalytic Association, Chicago, May 2000.

Eielson, J. E. (1955). "Cuerpo enamorado", in: Noche oscura del cuerpo. In: *Poesía Escrita* (p. 221). Bogotá: Editorial Norma, 1998.

Erikson, E. (1950). *Childhood and Society*. New York: Norton.

Erikson, E. H. (1966). *Identity and the Life Cycle*. New York: W. W. Norton.

Fain, M., & Marty, P. (1959). Aspects fonctionnels et role structurant de l'investissement homosexuel au cours de traitements psychanalytiques d'adultes. *Revue Française de Psychanalyse, 23*(5): 607–617.

Fast, I. (1979). Developments in gender identity: gender differentiation in girls. *International Journal of Psycho-Analysis, 60*(4): 443–454.

Fliess. (1906). *Der Ablauf des Lebens*. Leipzig-Wien: Franz Deuticke, 1906.

Freud, A. (1922). The relation of beating phantasies to a day-dream. *Int. J. Psycho-Anal.*, 4: 89–102, 1923.

Freud, A. (1925). Jealousy and desire of masculinity. In: *Opere Torino*. Bollati Boringhieri, 1978.

Freud, S. (1887–1904). *The Complete Letters of Sigmund Freud to Wilhelm Fliess*, J. M. Masson (Ed.). Harvard University Press, 1986.

Freud, S. (1900). The interpretation of dreams. *S.E.*, 4 and 5: xi–627.

Freud, S. (1901). Psychopathology of everyday life. *S.E.*, 6.

Freud, S. (1905). *Three Essays on the Theory of Sexuality. S.E.*, 7.

Freud, S. (1908). Hysterical phantasies and their relationship to bisexuality. *S.E.*, 9.

Freud, S. (1908 [1907]). Creative writing and day dreaming. *S.E.*, 9: 143–153.

Freud, S. (1909). Analysis of a phobia in a five-year-old boy. *S.E.*, 10: 3.

Freud, S. (1910). *A Special Type of Choice of Object made by Men (Contributions to the Psychology of Love I). S.E.*, 11: 165–175.

Freud, S. (1912). *On the Universal Tendency to Debasement in the Sphere of Love (Contributions to the Psychology of Love II). S.E.*, 5: 179–190.

Freud, S. (1914). On narcissism: an introduction. *S.E.*, 14.

Freud, S. (1919). A child is being beaten. *S.E.*, 17.

Freud, S. (1921). *Group Psychology and the Analysis of the Ego. S.E.*, 18.

Freud, S. (1923). *The Ego and the Id. S.E.*, 19: 3.

Freud, S. (1924a). *The Dissolution of the Oedipus Complex. S.E.*, 19: 173–179.

Freud, S. (1924b). *The Letters of Sigmund Freud and Karl Abraham: 1907–1926*. New York: Basic Books, 1965.

Freud, S. (1925). Some psychical consequences of the anatomical distinction between the sexes. *S.E.*, 19: 241–259.

Freud, S. (1933). *New Introductory Lectures on Psycho-Analysis. S.E.*, 22: 7–182.

Freud, S. (1937). *Analysis Terminable and Interminable. S.E.*, 23: 209–253.

Gaddini, E. (1969). Sulla Imitazione. In: *Scritti: 1953–1985*. Milano: R. Cortina Editore, 1989.

Gaddini, E. (1974). Formazione del padre e scena primaria. In: *Scritti 1953–1985*. Milano R. Cortina Editore, 1989.

Gay, P. (1988). *Freud. A Life for Our Time*. New York and London: W. W. Norton & Company.

Glocer de Fiorini, L. (2001). *Lo Femenino y el Pensamiento Complejo* (p. 154). Buenos Aires: Lugar Editorial.

Godfrind, J. (2001). *Comment la Féminité Vient aux Femmes*. Paris: PUF.

Green, A. (1975). *La Concepción Psicoanalítica del Afecto*. Spain: Siglo XXI Editores.

Green, A. (1993). La analidad primaria. In: *El Trabajo de lo Negativo*. Buenos Aires: Amorrortu Editores.

Green, A. (1995). *El Lenguaje en el Psicoanálisis*. Buenos Aires: Amorrortu Editores.

Greenson, R. R. (1968). Dis-identifying from mother: its special importance for the boy. *International Journal of Psycho-Analysis, 49*: 370–374.

Grossman, W. I. (1976). Discussion of "Freud and Female Sexuality". *International Journal of Psycho-Analysis, 57*: 301.

Guignard, F. (1989). Objet de transfert, oú est tu? *Revue Française de Psychanalyse, 53*(4): 1045–1054.

Haudenschild, T. (1994). Psiquê e suas vicissitudes: um mito sobre o desenvolvimento do feminino. Anais do XX Congresso da Fepal em Lima, Peru, Volume 3, p. 301.

Haudenschild, T. (1997). Retaking the first steps towards symbolisation: a 6-year-old emerges from adhesive identification. *International Journal of Psycho-Analysis, 78*: 733–753.

Haudenschild, T. (1999). El desvelar del habla. *Rivista de Psicoanalisi*, Numero Especial Intenacional 1998–1999 (6): 223–242.

Hoffman, I. Z. (1998). *Ritual and Spontaneity in the Psychoanalytic Process: A Dialectical–Constructivist View*. Hillsdale, NJ: The Analytic Press.

Hoffman, M. (1978). Sex differences in empathy and related behaviours. *Psychological Bulletin, 84*: 712–722.

Jordan, B. (1997). Gender, politics and infant mental health. *The Signal, 5*: 1–5.

Keiser, S. (1956). Female sexuality. *Journal of the American Psychoanalytic Association, 4*: 563–574.

Kestenberg, J. S. (1956). On the development of maternal feelings in early childhood: observation and reflections. *Psychoanalytic Study of the Child, 11*: 257–291.

Kestenberg, J. S. (1976). Regression and reintegration in pregnancy. *Journal of the American Psychoanalytic Association, 24*(suppl.): 213–250.

Klein, M. (1928). Early stages of the Oedipus conflict. In: *Love, Guilt and Reparation and Other Works. The Writings of Melanie Klein, Volume 1*. London: Karnac Books and the Institute of Psychoanalysis, 1992.

Klein, M. (1932a). The effects of the early anxiety-situations on the sexual development of the girl. In: *The Psycho-analysis of Children*. London: Hogarth, 1980.

Klein, M. (1932b). The psychoanalysis of children. In: *The Writings of Melanie Klein, Volume 2*. London: Karnac Books and the Institute of Psychoanalysis, 1986.

Koutas, M., & Federmeier, K. D. (1998). Minding the body. *Psychophysiology*, *35*: 135–150.

Kristeva, J. (1979). Women's time. In: T. Moi (Ed.), *The Kristeva Reader* (pp. 187–213). New York: Columbia University Press, 1986.

Kristeva, J. (1993). *Die neuen Leiden der Seele*. Hamburg: Junius, 1994.

Langer, M. (1953). *Motherhood and Sexuality*. New York: Guilford, 1992.

Lerner, H. (1976). Parental mislabeling of female genitals as a determinant of penis envy and learning inhibitions in women. *Journal of the American Psychoanalytic Association*, *24*(5): 269–285.

Leuzinger-Bohleber, M. (2001). The "Medea" fantasy: an unconscious determinant of psychogenic sterility. *International Journal of Psychoanalysis*, *82*: 323–345.

Lieberman, M. D. (2000). Intuition: A social cognitive neuroscience approach. *Psychological Bulletin*, *126*: 109–137.

McDougall, J. (1964). Considérations sur la relation d'objet dans l'homosexualité féminine. In: *Recherches Psychanalytiques sur la Sexualité Féminine*. Paris: Payot.

McDougall, J. (1996). *The Many Faces of Eros*. New York and London: W. W. Norton & Company.

Mitchel, J. (1986). The question of femininity and the theory of psychoanalysis. In: Gregorio Kohon (Ed.), *The British School of Psychoanalysis—The Independent Tradition*. London: Free Association Books, 1986.

Moromisato, D. (1988). A este cuerpo enamorado. En: *Morada donde la luna perdió su palidez* (p. 25). Lima: Cuarto Lima Editores.

Notman, M. T., & Lester, E. P. (1988). Pregnancy: theoretical considerations. *Psychoanalytic Inquiry*, *8*: 139–159.

Novelletto, A. (1991). *Psichiatria Psicoanalitica dell'Adolescenza*. Rome: Borla.

Perez-Sanches, M., & Abelio, N. (1980). Unité originaire. In: *Communications*. Congrès de Barcelone. Paris: PUF, 1980.

Pines, D. (1992). The relevance of early psychic development to pregnancy and abortion. *International Journal of Psycho-Analysis*, *63*: 311–319.

Pines, D. (1993). *A Woman's Unconscious Use of her Body*. London: Virago Press.

Poluda-Korte, E. (1993). Der "lesbische Komplex". Das homosexuelle Tabu und die Weiblichkeit. In: Eva M. Alvez (Ed.), *Stumme Liebe* (pp. 46–132). Freiburg: Kore.

Pontalis, J. B. (1982). El irascible a medias. In: *Bisexualidad y Diferencia de los Sexos*. Buenos Aires: Ediciones del 80.

Quinodoz, D. (1984). L'incapacité de bien traiter ses objets internes comme expression de l'homosexualité latente. *Revue Française de Psychanalyse*, 3: 745–750.

Quinodoz, D. (1990). L'insoutenable incertitude: le fantasme du berceau vide. *Revue Française de Psychanalyse*, 6: 1567–1572.

Quinodoz, D. (1993). L'angoisse de castration a-t-elle un équivalent féminin? *Revue Française de Psychanalyse*, 5: 1647–1572.

Quinodoz, D. (1994). *Le Vertige, entre Angoisse et Plaisir*. Paris: PUF [reprinted as *Emotional Vertigo, between Anxiety and Pleasure*. New York and London: Routledge].

Quinodoz, D. (2003). *Words That Touch: A Psychoanalyst Learns to Speak*. London: Karnac Books.

Raphael-Leff, J. (1993). *Pregnancy: The Inside Story*. London, UK: Sheldon Press.

Raphael-Leff, J. (2001). Panel on gender in the psychoanalytical method. *International Psychoanalytical Association Congress*, Nice.

Riedel, I. (1989). *Demeters Suche*. Zürich: Kreuz Verlag.

Rohde-Dachser, Ch. (1990). Über töchterliche existenz. In: *Psychosom. Med-u. Psychoanalyse*, 36, 303.

Rycroft, C. (1968). *Critical Dictionary of Psychoanalysis*. London: Thomas Nelson & Sons.

Salas, E. (1974). Aportes al estudio del papel de los padres en el desarrollo. *Rivista de Psicoanalisi*, 31(1–2): 403.

Salome, L. A. (1899). El ser humano como mujer. In: A. Mariam Alizade (Ed.), *Voces de Femineidad*. Buenos Aires, 1991.

Salome, L. A. (1914). *Il Tipo Femmina*. Milano: Minesis, 1992.

Siegel, D. J. (2001). Towards an interpersonal neurobiology of the developing mind: attachment relationships, "mindsight" and neural integration. *Infant Mental Health Journal*, 22: 67–94.

Spector Person, E. (1983). Women in therapy: therapist gender as a variable. *International Review of Psycho-Analysis*, 10: 193.

Spector Person, E. (1992). *The Erotic Transference and Countertransference in Women and in Men: Differences and Consequences*.

Spector Person, E. (1994). La "construcción" de la femineidad: su influencia a lo largo del ciclo de la vida. In: *Mujeres por Mujeres* (pp. 62–86). Lima: Moisés Lemlij Editor, Peruvian Library of Psychoanalysis.

Stern, D. (2000). Introduction. In: *The Interpersonal World of the Child*. New York: Basic Books.

Stoller, R. (1968). A further contribution to the study of gender identity. *International Journal of Psycho-Analysis, 49*: 364–368.

Stoller, R. (1968). *Sex and Gender*. New York: Science House.

Stoller, R. (1976). Primary femininity. *Journal of American Psychoanalytic Association, 24*(5): 59–78.

Stoller, R. (1979). *Sexual Excitement. Dynamics of Erotic Life*. London: Maresfield Library.

Stoller, R. (1986). *Dynamics of Erotic Life* (p. 205). London: Maresfield Library.

Szpilka, J. (1985). Edipo precoce, affetto retroattivo e conflitto psichico. *Rivista di Psicoanalisi, 30*: 5. Il Pensiero Scientifico Editore.

Wallerstein, R. (1973). Psychoanalytic perspectives on the problem of reality. *Journal of American Psychoanalytic Association, 21*: 5–33.

Weininger, O. (1903). *Sesso e Carattere*. Roma: Edizioni Mediterranee, 1992 [original version: *Geschlecht und Character*. Vienna–Lipsia: Braumüller, 1903].

Winnicott, D. W. (1951). Transitional objects and transitional phenomena. *Through Paediatrics to Psycho-Analysis*. New York: Basic Books, 1958.

Winnicott, D. W. (1956). On transference. *International Journal of Psycho-Analysis, 37*: 386–388.

Winnicott, D. W. (1971). *Playing and Reality*. London: Tavistock Publications.

Winnicott, D. W. (1988). *Human Nature*. London: The Winnicott Trust.

Wisdom, J. O. (1983). Man and Woman. *International Journal of Psycho-Analysis, 2*.

Zak de Goldstein, R. (1997). *De la Erótica. Un Estudio Psicoanalítico de la Sexualidad Femenina*. Argentina: Ediciones Publikar.